DETOUR BERLIN

DETOUR BERLIN

Ruth Baja Williams

To order additional copies of this book, contact:

Xlibris Corporation

1-888-7-XLIBRIS

www.Xlibris.com

Orders@Xlibris.com

12184

CONTENTS

This book is dedicated to Charles.

PROLOGUE

I never intended to go to Berlin. It was the furthest thing from my mind at age twenty-two. I was only vaguely aware of where Berlin was. It was somewhere in Germany, somewhere in that other Germany, East Germany, tucked away behind the Iron Curtain and inaccessible to the likes of me. Anyway, there was so much else in the world to see. I had already crossed the Pacific twice, lived on three continents, in several countries, but I longed to go to Europe. In my mind, that meant visiting capital cities such as London, Paris, Rome, Amsterdam, Brussels, Zurich. Not Berlin.

I set out on my first voyage at age two and a half with my mother, father, brother, and aunt. We left the Philippines, our homeland, in October 1941, just six weeks before Japanese planes dropped bombs on Pearl Harbor. My father had a scholarship to study international relations at the University of Southern California. Like so many ambitious, young Protestant Filipino intellectuals, he had visions of a better life for his family in America, that great and generous country that had freed his land from 300 years of oppression by Catholic Spain. His vision for my brother and me was to prove to the world that we Filipinos could be as American as any American. We could speak as Americans, behave as Americans—contribute positively to the good of American society.

When we left our home on Oregon Street in the Malate District of Manila to take the ship for America, we carried only clothing and family photos. We had sold everything else, "down to the last teaspoon," as my mother would tell me later. There followed a tearful scene of farewell at dockside, a scene I would hear about often in the years to come. The retelling would stir baby memories of pressing crowds of well-wishing relatives and friends, of wet cheeks against mine and snuffles and sniffs—long inhaling sniffs of goodbye, the Filipino way, rather than puckered-lip kisses on my cheeks. Aboard the *SS President Coolidge*, we rode steerage like the other immigrants to America, the land of unlimited promise.

Ruth at two and a half aboard the *SS President Coolidge*

We rented a small house in Los Angeles where we would live while my father attended classes at the University of Southern California. Soon after our arrival, America entered World War II, and we were issued red, white, and blue tin badges with the words "I am Filipino." Our Japanese and Japanese-American neighbors were rounded up and sent to internment camps, their heritage alone branding them as the enemy, while our little tin badges proclaimed to the world that we were Asians who were fighting the Japanese just as hard as our tall American brothers.

Of those early years in America, I remember crowded, laughter-filled weekends with my family and members of the Filipino community. My shiny Mary Janes patent leather shoes slid on polished floors, and my cheeks were constantly grabbed by affectionate "aunties" and "uncles."

"Aba! [Imagine that!] She sounds just like an American," they'd say. Then astonishment became tinged with sadness. "She doesn't speak Tagalog?"

"No," beamed my parents. How proud they were of their American-sounding daughter. They had plans for me to return to the Philippines with the best foreign education they could afford. I would speak English without a trace of a Filipino accent. Later, I could always learn Tagalog, the most widely spoken of the Philippines' eighty-seven languages.

News of the Japanese takeover of the Philippines reached us, and young male classmates left Dad's university courses and joined the United States Army. Then Dad had a chance to serve both his native country and America, the land of his new, fiercely burning loyalty. He was recruited by the Office of War Information to broadcast messages in Tagalog that were beamed across the Pacific to the Philippines. They exhorted his fellow Filipinos to hold fast and stand firm against the Japanese invasion, for the United States was building an unbeatable military force and arsenal and would soon come to their aid.

The broadcasting job took our family 385 miles north to San Francisco. Sometimes I would accompany Dad to the studio, where I was allowed to sit in the control booth. The big American broadcasting people were always very kind and winked at me broadly. "Watch the big second hand, honey. When it reaches twelve, your dad will start to speak."

After the war, the Philippines were granted independence from the United States, and the Philippine diplomatic corps was established. On hearing that candidates for the new corps were being sought, Dad applied. His application was accepted, and he was sent to Washington, D.C., for training.

In June 1948, our family crossed the Pacific once more. This time, six and a half years after the first crossing, we were on board the *SS President Wilson*. This time, we were in first class, traveling westward from Los Angeles back to Manila.

The wharf from which we had departed in 1941 was a shambles. The scars of war were everywhere in the city. All that was left of the house on Oregon Street were three concrete steps that led to an empty lot where the rubble had been cleared away and weeds grew high and free. The house, whose image my baby memories could not conjure up, was completely gone and with it all trace of my beginnings.

After a six-week stay in Manila, my family and I took our first airplane flight to Hong Kong, where Dad was assigned to the Philippine Consulate and where I would attend Diocesan Girls' School, a Chinese school.

I made no friends in that Hong Kong school. Except for the uniform I and all the other day girls wore, I had nothing in common with anyone. At lunchtime, I munched on my peanut butter and jelly sandwich, while the Chinese girls, each with an attending amah (maid), were pampered and fed by chopsticks, their lips wiped clean, and their brows cooled with a damp cloth. I sat silent, alone, watching, feeling neither envy nor disdain for I was outside of their world.,

A special Chinese language class for non-Chinese was held for two British girls, two girls from India, and me. I looked almost like the girls from Hong Kong, but I did not know their language, and I became aware that my English was different from the English spoken by the British and Indian girls. Despite the class, I didn't learn much Chinese that year; at most I could help my mother haggle with a peddler selling trinkets from bamboo baskets on the street.

Our apartment was one floor above street level on Prince Edward Road in Kowloon, the peninsula on mainland China that was part of the British Crown Colony. From our wraparound verandah, we could watch vehicular and foot traffic below. In 1949 and 1950, foot traffic doubled, quadrupled, then increased ten-fold, as refugees arrived, fleeing China before the advancing armies of Mao Zedong. The sidewalk below our apartment filled with humanity. Families took up residence in the space beneath the stairs leading from the ground floor as the world outside became more and more crowded. Whenever we left our apartment, we had to pick our way carefully between people sitting, sleeping, and eating before we finally reached the car.

One evening I heard Mom and Dad talking in low and worried voices. Dad was being sent to the Philippine Consulate in Amoy, a port city in the southeast of mainland China. Mom was weeping, disconsolate at the possibility of our being separated from him or of us all being trapped in that city as it was overrun by Communist forces. Fortunately, Mao and his army arrived in the city before we left Hong Kong, and the Philippine Department of Foreign Affairs sent Dad to Sydney, Australia, instead.

In our new home in Vaucluse, an upper-middle-class suburb on the eastern end of Sydney, my mother gave beautiful dinner parties. She'd hire a bartender and a maid to help in the kitchen. I was not allowed to help in the kitchen because my pretty dress should not be soiled. My job was to fill with nuts the small, dainty, porcelain dishes that stood beside each place setting. In our formal dining room in Sydney, I would see my father at his histrionic finest, jabbing a forefinger at a linen serviette that represented a telegram. (I had learned to say "serviette"as the Australians did, not "napkin," the word I had learned in America.) Dad held the "cable" aloft in his other hand, declaring, "We were about to go to Amoy, but the Communists were just a hundred miles away. Orders for my transfer came on the day Amoy fell to the Red Army. I received a cable on one day and a second one the next. The first one said, 'Proceed to Amoy.' The second one said, 'Disregard first cable—stop—you are being transferred to Sydney.' We just missed being trapped by one day—by golly!" He sat down, flushed with the drama of it all, while the dinner guests nodded in reverent appreciation of their host's marvelous escape.

By then, my father was first secretary and consul general at the Philippine Legation in Sydney. My mother was enjoying much attention in the society pages of Sydney's newspapers. My brother and I were in private schools. I was in fifth grade (or fifth form, as they called it there), working hard to learn long division in pounds, shillings, and pence, and British, rather than American, spelling, and, more importantly, to unlearn American pronunciation and expressions. When I wrote "I have gotten" in a composition, instead of "I have received," it was crossed out with a vicious "Americanism!" exclaimed in the margin. It was clear to me that my teachers did not like things American. The daughter of a Philippine diplomat should not sound like a Yank.

When Dad's transfer to Indonesia came, we packed up the house in Vaucluse, the home we had known for three years, boarded the *Nieuw Holland*, and sailed for the capital city of Djakarta on December 28, 1952. Rounding the northern tip of York Peninsula on New Year's Eve, we celebrated New Year's Day 1953 five times. The ship, sailing due west, was catching up to and passing the midnight hour again and again. Each time midnight was celebrated with the clanking of bells and cheers by an increasingly inebriated crew, until finally, midnight was left behind in the ship's wake, and all was quiet.

The entire summer vacation (December to February in the southern hemisphere) was spent at the Hotel des Indes, in Djakarta, where my brother and I hooked up with a group of unattached teenage internationals. We'd meet at four in the afternoon, when the worst of the tropical heat had abated, and walk together, some pushing bikes, and talk and talk—in English. There were a brother and a sister from London (who beat my brother and me soundly on the tennis court most mornings), two sisters from Helsinki, and four Indonesian youths. We were friends, united by being young people speaking English.

In February, my brother and I flew back Sydney for the beginning of the school year. My brother was in his first year at Sydney

University. I was placed as a boarder in Methodist Ladies' College (MLC), Burwood, an inner western suburb of Sydney. It was an eighteen-hour trip by propeller plane: eight from Djakarta to Darwin, the capital of Australia's Northern Territory, then another ten from Darwin to Sydney. The four-engine propeller plane served hot meals with silverware and glassware. The overhead space was not for storage but could fold down to form a bed; the seat below unfolded flat for a lower bunk. There was plenty of airsickness, but no jet lag. For the next four years, my brother and I would make the commute between Indonesia and Australia at the end and the beginning of every antipodean summer.

When I first arrived at MLC, the students there asked me, the new girl, Where are you from? I live in Djakarta now. What's it like there? Do they have houses like we do? I don't know it very well. I've only lived there for six weeks. Oh. And they'd turn away in wonder at this person who didn't know anything about home.

By now I was speaking Australian with only a slight American accent. On hikes, I was the girl who knew all the words to "Waltzing Matilda," because I thought everyone had to know them. Without understanding why, I was swept along in heartfelt devotion to the Australian World War I heroes of Gallipoli, and I knew by heart the map of the world where all the countries in red belonged to the British Empire—on which the sun never set.

In Australia, I made close friends (with whom I am in contact to this day), but the beautiful country down under, my home of seven years, where I had been the recipient of wonderful kindness, would not have me for a citizen in 1956 when I finished secondary school. Australia still held to a White Australia Policy, which banned immigrants who were not Caucasian, and I would never be white.

In December 1956, I flew to Los Angeles. Ah, back home— sort of. But my speech and accent were once more a handicap to my fitting in. Now I sounded like an Australian—or, as was often stated, "something British." And in the 1950s, Asians in California (we were called Orientals then) who sounded British were rare and regarded with curiosity. My first job, therefore, was to un-learn British and pick up American speech once more. I didn't wish to stand out.

Ruth in the uniform of Methodist Ladies' College Burwood

Ahead of me lay four years of undergraduate studies. Then my plan was to travel around for a few months. After that, I'd settle in the States. I, who had no roots anywhere, would be sure to find a home in the United States of America. That was my father's vision, and it was mine, too.

In 1957, the Russians launched Sputnik, the first man-made earth satellite. I was a freshman at Los Angeles City College. On hearing the news of Sputnik's launch, I felt the earth go soft under my feet. Something was circling around the whole earth! And the world had suddenly become a smaller place. Beep-beep! Beep-beep! Sputnik said. The world was changing.

A year later, an event just as momentous for me, personally, occurred: I met Charles. My journalism course required me to interview a singer at a lunchtime student recital. Charles, a voice and drama major, was singing Italian art songs, and I was taking notes. We fell in love. I can't remember how it happened; I only know that it did. We fell in love so suddenly, so rapidly, and so completely that it seemed the whole progression of events was wrested from our hands and arranged by forces outside ourselves. Anyone who has ever been truly in love will know exactly what I mean. We were foolishly, madly, utterly in love. We were nuts and blind and totally besotted with one another. All I knew for sure about anything was that when I was with him, I was happy. I was home.

"But Ruth, he's Negro!" Charles was a Negro—so what? Why did college classmates sound as if they were warning me of something? Fortunately, our mutual friends didn't seem to care; they said we made such a cute couple. The Civil Rights Movement was gaining momentum, but we cared not a bit about the social upheavals rumbling around us or breaking out in demonstrations. While other college students were holding cafeteria sit-ins in Atlanta, we lingered in a small jazz café in Hollywood called Bit of Europe, where Les McCann at the piano, Leroy Vinegar on bass and Ron Harrison on drums improvised for hours. We walked hand in hand in Griffith Park or sat on the swing of the cool porch behind the bungalow of Charles's great-aunt Johnnie, who was always kind and welcoming. She looked at us one day, smiled bravely, and said, "Well, at least, you're both Methodist."

Aunt Johnnie, with her gray-blue eyes, rosy cheeks, and light brown hair, was fairer than I. She was a gentle woman seasoned to a beautiful glow by experience. On trains in the segregated South, she once told me, colored porters begged her to *please* move to the carriages for the white folks so they, the porters, would not get into trouble for placing a white lady in the wrong carriage. She always assured them that she was sitting right where she belonged. She was careful to explain to me that she and her family were colored. I was not to use the term *Negro*. (The label *black* was just coming into use, and *African-American* had not yet been devised.)

Aunt Johnnie gave me a lot to think about, opening the Pandora's box of racism to me, the privileged little diplomat's daughter whose separateness had been to my advantage. But I was too crazy in love to bother thinking clearly about anything ponderous for long. I was dancing in youthful, happy abandon: free, strong, immutable, immortal.

In 1959, Charles decided to drop out of college for one semester to perform in an all-black musical called *Carnival Island* at the all-black theater Ebony Showcase in Los Angeles, following his dreams of a career on stage. "It might go to Broadway," he said with a faraway smile. I found it wonderful to be in the company of a young man who knew exactly where he wanted to go. In Los Angeles, many potential angels viewed the musical *Carnival Island,* but promises in 1960 to bring the production to Broadway were never realized. Broadway was not quite ready for an all-black show. The U.S. Army, however, was ready with another plan for Charles, who no longer had his college deferment. He was swiftly drafted into service and sent to Ford Ord, California, for basic training, and then to Ft. Riley, Kansas.

That summer of 1960, while Charles was at Fort Ord, I sailed by Japanese freighter from San Francisco to Tokyo to visit my parents. My father was then chargé d'affaires at the Philippine Embassy in Tokyo.

Charles had given me an eight-by-ten-inch black-and-white photo of himself in dress uniform. I thought he looked swell. As I was unpacking my suitcase, my mother saw Charles's photo, and a look of horror crossed her face.

Charles in dress uniform

"He's just a friend, Mom," I said, sensing that there might be conflict ahead, and put the photo away.

She said nothing, but I could tell by her frown that her stomach had twisted itself into a tight knot. Later I would hear my mom and dad in the adjacent room, arguing over what to do about Ruthie. The next morning they confronted me. "We think you are secretly engaged."

"No, we are just dating."

My mother burst into tears and clung to me. "Your children will be ugly! They will be dark!" she wailed.

To say the least, my parents were not pleased with my romantic attachment. They were caught in that no-man's-land between theory and reality for they had carefully taught me not to judge a person by race but by integrity and acts of kindness. Here I was, following their teaching, and suddenly their beautiful idealism was beginning to quake.

My mother's initial outburst aside, my parents' criticism was communicated not so much in words as in a cold silence that pulled at the gut. Fortunately for me, my flight back to Los Angeles left three hours early to avoid a typhoon bearing down on Honshu. The god of mercy and great storms was releasing me from my mother's arms.

In the fall, I began my second semester as a senior at the University of Southern California, where I soon received a letter from Charles saying he was being sent to Augsburg, West Germany. "I'm going to Europe!" Charles's letter in my hand vibrated with his excitement. "I've always wanted to go to Europe." So have I, I thought. Jealousy tugged down the corners of my mouth.

We continued our romance by airmail. I waxed eloquent and poetic, creating on paper a world of high hope, love, and laughter. In one of Charles's letters, he asked me to marry him. And my shortest letter to him was in swift reply: Yes.

But first! First there was Europe to see: London, Paris, Rome. I had to get that in. I had to keep my promise to myself. After Charles's two-year army stint, after we came back to the States, when would I ever see Europe again? I would have my tour. On my way to the altar, I would see all those European capitals.

CHAPTER 1

Finding a Temporary Home

The desire to travel in Europe was widespread. People talked wistfully about going there someday. At my first job after college graduation, I met a young woman named Joanne who wished more than anything to go to Europe. Quite simply and easily, we planned a trip together.

Three days and two nights on a Greyhound bus took us from Los Angeles to New Orleans, where we boarded the *Charles Lykes*, a freighter bound for Liverpool. From Liverpool to Oxford, we hitchhiked, then thumbed our way on to London, where we walked and walked, ran in and out of Harrods, went to the show at the Palladium, took pictures of each other, and marked items off our list of things we had to see.

To save the cost of a hotel room, we spent our last night in London on the wooden benches at Victoria Station, then boarded the ferry for the Hook of Holland. In Brussels, I bought my wedding veil. In Amsterdam, I bought little porcelain clogs.

On August 13, 1961, we were sightseeing in Paris. We were so charmed by the city on the Seine that we paid no attention to the newspaper headlines about a border being closed to stem the flow of refugees streaming by the thousands into West Berlin from East Berlin. That great central European metropolis was of no interest to us. It did not fit into our European mantra—London-Paris-Rome. We made sure that we saw the *Venus de Milo*, and the *Mona Lisa* at the Louvre; then we went up the Eiffel Tower, imagining that we heard the haunting strains of an accordion being played just around the next corner as we ascended.

Despite screaming headlines, we were oblivious to the news that barbed wire was being strung along the east-west border cutting through the heart of Berlin and that people were being lowered over it from apartment windows in the eastern zone into the welcoming arms of people on the street below in the western zone. I knew nothing of these events, and even if I had stopped to read about them, I would not have understood.

As the Wall was being built in Berlin, all U.S. forces in the city and in West Germany, including Charles, my husband-to-be, were put on alert standing. American troops were told that one battle group, no one yet knew which, would be sent to West Berlin to augment the U.S. garrison already there. Charles was no longer sure that he would still be in Augsburg for our wedding in September.

From Paris, Joanne and I took a train to Rome. In Vatican City we stared up at the ceiling of the Sistine Chapel, which was veiled now in the gloom of inadequate light and not spread out on a brilliant broad screen as it had been in "A Survey of Art History 101."

On August 20, 1961, President John F. Kennedy ordered the First Battle Group of the 18th Infantry—not Charles's unit—from West Germany across the Berlin-Helmsted Autobahn through East Germany to U.S.-occupied West Berlin. On that same day, Joanne and I were on a train traveling to Zurich. And in Augsburg, Charles remained on alert.

From Zurich, Joanne and I traveled to Munich and then to Augsburg. When our train pulled into the station on September 1, Charles was there to greet us with two bouquets of flowers.

"He's wonderful," said Joanne, her eyes shining.

"I know."

How simple and easy was our wedding. No fuss, no crowds, no aunts and uncles traveling miles for the occasion. Only Joanne and I had come from far away. Only Joanne and Charles were not strangers to me.

Of course Joanne would be my bridesmaid, for we had become good friends. We had discussed the matter in Los Angeles. Joanne was from a Polish family in Chicago and a devout Roman Catholic. She said she would ask the army priest in Augsburg for permission. I did not understand her internal struggle as we traveled together. She insisted on visiting at least one cathedral in every city along our journey from Los Angeles to Augsburg. She would always light a candle, kneel for long fervent minutes, then tell me, "I prayed for your wedding."

Father Murphy, the U.S. Army priest in Augsburg, said it was not right for Joanne to be a bridesmaid at a Protestant wedding and refused her permission. Joanne was hurt and saddened, especially because I couldn't understand her predicament, but she remained obedient to the priest's words. So a sergeant's daughter whom I had met a few days before the ceremony would don a pretty pink dress and walk ahead of me down the aisle. On writing this almost four decades later, I can't even remember her name.

I had told my parents, who were now assigned to the Philippine Embassy in Seoul, Korea, of my plans. Over several months leading up to my wedding day, I had written to them a constant stream of letters praising Charles, telling them how they would love him if they would just meet him. But they chose not to make the long journey from Seoul to Augsburg. "You will be divorced in two years," my mother had predicted in a letter. But I was determined to prove her wrong.

Charles was a chaplain's assistant and enjoyed great popularity on base. On our wedding day, his many friends and acquaintances filled the Centerville Chapel on Reese Kaserne, outside of the ancient city of Augsburg. One of Charles's army buddies was the best man. Charles's four barracks roommates, wearing white carnations in their narrow lapels, acted as ushers, and later his platoon sergeant stood in my father's stead and accompanied me down the aisle. The Protestant Women of the Chapel arranged our wedding reception, the infantry commander's wife served punch, and it seemed to me that almost everyone—except Charles and me—

cried. I wondered then whether they thought that a marriage such as ours was doomed to failure and that was why they cried. I wanted to tell them all not to cry. We would make this marriage work, we really would. Whatever walls or barriers might stand in the way of a happy life would eventually be crossed, breached, broken through, brought down. The world was a wonderful place. It always is for people who are young and very much in love.

Meanwhile, a city less than 200 miles away, a city I had yet to meet, was in turmoil. In East Berlin, the barbed wire barrier was being thickened by cinder blocks and mortar. People whose homes were on the eastern side of the East-West sector line were being evicted. Would-be escapees could no longer jump or be lowered from apartment windows into the West. The crisis in Berlin was worsening.

Charles and I spent our weekend honeymoon in a one-room country cottage a half hour's drive from Augsburg. A female Polish doctor lived in the cottage next door. She performed a little ceremony of greeting, presenting us with two slices of bread, two small glasses of water, and a tiny heap of salt, all carefully arranged on a silver tray. In halting, thickly accented English, she spoke earnestly, explaining that this gift would ensure that we would always have enough food and drink. She wished us good fortune and a life without war or suffering.

We placed a pinch of salt on the bread, ate it, then drank the water. And the good doctor, overwhelmed by the moment, burst into tears. She pulled from her apron pocket a large hanky, with which she smothered her sobs. It was then that I noticed the tattooed concentration camp numbers on her arm.

We said goodbye to Joanne, who was returning to the United States the following week. I settled into my new life, which included wonderful new friends such as Lutz, a young German who worked the lights in some of the army's theater productions. Before my arrival, Lutz had often invited Charles and other GI buddies for Sunday afternoon coffee and cake at his home in downtown Augsburg, where he lived with his parents, whom everybody

called Mama and Papa. Charles had spent many Sunday afternoons with Mama and Papa. He had felt comfortable and welcome in their home, and, released for a few hours from the pres-
sures of army life, he had often fallen asleep on their living-room
couch. Now I was invited, too, and I discovered that Mama made
the tastiest plum cobbler I had ever eaten.

I was delighted with my life. I was married. My husband's
friends were like brothers, and we even had a mama and a papa.
The newness of everything was exhilarating. I was eager to learn all
I could about this new country, new culture, new language. I'd
drink in the music, the museums, the beautiful countryside. It
didn't matter that our relatives were so far away. Now I belonged
with my husband. Wherever he was, was where I, too, belonged.
Someday soon we'd go back to the United States; I'd become an
American citizen. We'd have hybrid children who, as everyone
knows, would be more beautiful, smarter, and healthier than offspring of same race parents. And, obviously, they would be accepted everywhere. The Civil Rights Movement was making ad-
vances and things could only get better. Right? I did not imagine
then that my life was about to take a lengthy detour from the
planned itinerary.

In the third week of November 1961, we heard that the men
were going to Berlin. Reese Kaserne was suddenly buzzing with
activity. The chaplain, firm lipped, whispered, "Make sure Ruth
has enough fuel for the winter," but Charles told me nothing of
this.

All dependents of the First Battle Group of the 19th Infantry,
stationed in Augsburg, West Germany, were summoned to the
movie house on Flak Kaserne for a briefing by the base commander,
Col. Ira Palm. I was jostled by diaper bags and giant teddy bears as
I entered the dimly lit movie house with the other dependent
women and their children. I had to watch my step or a little stroller
wheel might run over my foot. We were curious, murmuring and
wondering, surprised at the serious tone of the summons. Col.

Palm, a tall, fatherly figure, told us how proud we should be that our men were about to serve in the "Outpost City of West Berlin."

In the hushed theater's twilight, a baby cried and a toddler fussed.

"Our battle group moves out next week," announced the commander.

There was a collective gasp, followed by nervous chatter.

"Sir?" A woman raised her hand. "How long will our men be away?"

"That," answered the commander, "we do not know." Then someone fainted, and those around her turned to offer aid.

We were dismissed, and the chatter around me rose loudly. " . . . going home . . . he's due to rotate in three months." "Who knows how long this will be . . ." " . . . baby's coming in eight weeks, better get home as soon as possible . . . can't be together anyway."

Just nine weeks before, I had arrived in Augsburg to marry Charles, and now he would be leaving, and the commander could not say how long his army unit would be away. Many women were going home. Where was home for me? Where could I go? I was not an American citizen. I had no family in the States. My parents were in Seoul; my brother had immigrated to Canada. I had just found a home. My husband was my home. Now he was being sent away. Where was this West Berlin, anyway, this city that was taking away my husband? Berlin was not on my list of European capitals.

On December 4, 1961, Charles and the First Battle Group of the 19th Infantry were on their way to West Berlin. I had not yet found Berlin on a map. I could not yet grasp the significance of the phrase "110 miles behind the Iron Curtain." All I really could understand was that Charles was gone.

It is not my nature to stay quiet for long. Wasn't I an adventurer, an explorer? Now alone in our apartment on the outskirts of Augsburg, I announced to the emptiness around me, "I will learn

German!" It would be something to do, something to fill the days. German might be useful someday, I thought.

At the Army Education Center, I signed up for beginning German class, where I discovered sixteen ways to say *the* and fifteen possibilities of making a mistake just saying *the*! I battled with relative pronouns that masqueraded as definite articles. I memorized grammar charts containing words that sounded like "damn it" and "vomit," and I guessed pathetically at word endings that would remain a mystery to me forever.

On my own, I explored Augsburg. Sometimes I would go to the open marketplace where short, round women wore bandanas and many skirts. The older ones looked like the grandmother who lived on the ground floor of our house. Jolly and fat, they were hawking their goods in words I could not understand. None of the sounds they made matched anything I was learning in German class. I stared at them as intently as they stared at me, for we had never seen the likes of one another before. They set out their produce in meticulous rows: tomatoes, cabbages, apples. Potatoes and eggs were built into tidy pyramids. I took great delight in buying just one potato and one apple, one tomato and one egg, because it was fun to buy in such small quantities.

One morning two weeks after Charles's departure, I lay in bed, vaguely aware that I had been awake for some time. There was a strangeness about the morning light that I was struggling to identify through my sleepiness. It seemed brighter than on other mornings, but so much quieter. There was no sound of an occasional car passing in the street below. Even the twitter of birds was absent.

I put my arm out from under the blankets and turned on our little transistor radio, which we had constantly tuned to the American Forces Network. An AFN announcer was saying, " . . . last night's heavy snowfall. Repeat: All dependent high schools and elementary schools in the Augsburg and Munich areas are canceled for the day due to last night's heavy snowfall." I blinked at the ceiling. Except for a few white patches on distant mountains outside Los Angeles, I had never seen snow. Snow! I jumped out of bed and ran barefoot to the window.

For minutes I stood gaping in wonder at the beauty that met my eyes. Across the street the fields that yesterday were green and brown were now one huge blanket of white. The pine trees along the road, which I had hardly noticed in the busy weeks behind me, had changed as if by magic into Christmas trees, decorated now by sparkling snow. And the picket fence just below my window stood like a row of proud little soldiers, each wearing a clean white hat.

I shrieked my joy at the picture before me. I had to get out into that wonderland to experience fully what my eyes beheld. I threw on a pair of jeans, a sweater, and some tennis shoes and hurried down the three flights of stairs to the outside.

The snow greeted me as I opened the front door. I stepped off the front porch and looked down at my feet. They had disappeared into ankle-deep snow. And then the cold hit me. My feet were colder than I had ever known before. This time my scream was pain. Blindly, I ran back upstairs. I pulled off my wet shoes and sat down to ponder this new phenomenon.

The cold, the sheer coldness of everything—the icy wind, the slippery streets, the freezing apartment—would become my constant enemy. We had a woodstove for heating and cooking, and there was a basket of kindling outside the kitchen door. But I'd never been a Girl Scout and never been to camp. I had only a vague idea of how to make a fire. The grandma of the family that lived on the first and second floors came up one day to show me how to make a fire in the woodstove that was our heater. Make a small fire, yes you can use matches, add kindling; not too much or you'll smother the fire. Not too little or the fire will go out. I tried and tried, but couldn't get the hang of it. The fire kept dying. And, of course, I couldn't figure out how to keep the fire going under the water heater attached to the bathtub four floors down in the basement either.

Fortunately, I met a young nurse in my German class who helped me solve my fire-making problems. She was tall and freckled, with a head of thick red hair. She followed me out of class one day, staring. Hesitantly, she asked what part of China I was from. "I'm not Chinese. I'm Filipino." I heard the apology in my voice and felt that old familiar embarrassment about not really being a Filipino. She would ask me something about the Philippines, and I wouldn't know the answer. She said I was small boned like the Chinese from the north of China but dark skinned like the people from the south of China. I was not Chinese, I assured her, I was Filipino. (Sort of, I thought. At least that's what my passport said.)

We became fast friends. Eleanor, who worked at the U.S. Army hospital, had been born in China and lived there until she was seventeen. Five foot seven and fair, she was what we nowadays might call a typical Anglo-American, but her gait and the gentle sway of her body bespoke another culture. She was so very Asian in her thinking and manners, while I was so very Western, despite my ninety-four pounds, five foot height, and long straight black hair. It was as though we were the opposites of each other.

Learning of my fire-making difficulties, Eleanor offered to let me use her bathtub; I gladly accepted. After German class, we'd have supper together in her BOQ, bachelor officers' quarters, near the Army Education Center. She'd go on duty from midnight to 7:00 *A.M.* while I slept in her bed. Then I'd get up, and she'd slip between the still warm sheets. I'd catch the trolley to the edge of town, then walk along the road leading to Steppach, a small village outside of Augsburg, until I reached home.

It got so cold in my apartment one night that the water pipe under the sink broke. I spent hours mopping up and squeezing out freezing water into a bucket and, when it got full, dumping the water into the toilet on the landing. The leak never stopped. I gave up in exhaustion around 2:00 *A.M.* and went to bed. Later that morning, Grandma was in my kitchen whacking away at the woodstove, and by the afternoon, a small, new oil heater had been installed. To have a warm living space, all I had to do now was pour oil into the heater and light it. I was in heaven and wrote a glowing account of my trial by ice to Charles in Berlin.

I told the sergeant in charge of dependent wives that I needed heating oil for my new stove. He loaded two empty ten-gallon drums into a jeep, and together we rode to a military gas station to have them filled. Happily, we bumped along the country road outside of Augsburg, to the house where my freezing, lonely little home occupied the top floor. On the way, I kept smelling gasoline. "Are you sure this is heating oil? It sure smells like gasoline to me." The sergeant seemed not to hear me. He was a short-timer, he said. Four days and a wake up, and he'd be heading back to the good ole U.S. of A. I listened, then caught another whiff of gasoline. "Are you sure that's oil? It smells like gas. It smells like gas. It smells like gas." The sergeant slowed down. He looked at me like I was some sort of puzzle. He scratched his head. He frowned. His head seemed to be busy undoing a set of knots. He turned the jeep around and went to a German gas station, "on the economy" as military folks used to say when purchasing items from German merchants and not from the Post Exchange. I watched him do some fast and fancy bargaining with the man there. Saying nothing to me, the sergeant unloaded the two suspicious smelling drums. Then, after adding some dollars to the transaction, he brought two other drums to the jeep. That night, I quietly struck a match to light my new oil heater and enjoyed a warm little home.

My days weren't only spent learning German and trying to stay warm, of course. Sometimes I took the trolley into downtown Augsburg to visit Mama on Stettin Strasse. When I was told I would be allowed to visit Charles in Berlin over Christmas, Mama said we should make Christmas cookies that, I could take them to Charles and his friends. We mixed and rolled and cut the cookies while warm fragrances of cinnamon, ginger, and almond filled the spacious, high ceilinged, drafty kitchen. Mama's ample figure bent patiently over the trays of cookies as they came out of the oven. She fussed over them and decorated them as if she were dressing a crowd of quiet children. Lovingly, Mama smiled back at the gingerbread men whose smiling faces she had just painted. Meticulously, Mama placed tiny candies on the cookies in tidy designs, while I impatiently tossed candy sprinkles on rows of cooling cookies and called it a day.

Sometimes Papa came home from work while I was still baking cookies with Mama. He was a thin man. Everything about him was spare. His graying hair was slicked straight back from his forehead. His eyes were keen, his cheeks hollow, and his cheek bones prominent. The first thing he did after he'd taken off his coat was light a cigarette and sit down with the evening paper. He was full of laughter and sayings which I knew must be witty for his eyes danced. When he told jokes, he enjoyed them more than his hearers. For my benefit, he spoke slowly and carefully: A mouse and an elephant went to the priest. The priest said, "You two want to marry?" Papa looked up to a tall imaginary elephant and then down to a tiny imaginary mouse. Then Papa said in a high squeaky mouse voice: "Not want to marry—we have to marry!" Papa erupted into gales of laughter, unconsciously crumpling the evening newspaper in his mirth. I laughed, too, because he was having such a good time. Then Mama set an Abendbrot (an evening meal of bread and cold cuts) on the coffee table and sent us to wash our hands for supper.

Not long after my baking session with Mama, I boarded a bus to Frankfurt with other army dependents for the first leg of our journey to Berlin. I felt grateful that my name was on the list of wives who would be in Berlin with our husbands over Christmas. We traveled along snow-covered roads through tall pine forests whose branches were heavily laden with snow. In Frankfurt, we boarded the duty train to West Berlin.

During the first part of the trip, we were constantly being briefed, constantly warned of the danger zone we were about to enter. We would be traveling at night through East Germany. If the train stopped, we were not to speak to anyone outside the train, for this was enemy territory, the Communist world. We were not even to raise the window blinds and look out. We would be traveling through the night. Stern-faced young soldiers delivered these directives in stilted voices that seemed not to be their own. It was terribly mysterious. It seemed somewhat dangerous, but I shrugged off the seriousness of it because somehow I didn't believe it.

Between Christmas and March, I made two visits to Berlin (visits to Berlin for army dependents were scheduled every four weeks). During those visits, I met Mama's sister Susi and Susi's husband, Werner. Susi was a younger, slimmer version of Mama. But the generosity was the same. How wonderful were the great cakes baked for afternoon coffees. Like Mama's apartment, Tante Susi's smelled of warm baking goodies, shelter, safety, and love.

Onkel Werner was a shining, smiling man with ruddy cheeks and thinning hair. He was always busy fixing this or that, working at his desk, arranging his address cards, writing letters, sorting slides, getting things in order. But he'd stop promptly when Susi called him to the table for a meal.

Charles and I adored our times together in Berlin, of course, but while apart we kept busy. In Augsburg, I was going to German class and exploring my surroundings. Meanwhile, Charles was discovering a city of music and theater in Berlin, a city he'd been drawn to from the beginning. On entering West Berlin, his unit had been greeted by cheering crowds and people throwing flowers. Charles had felt so welcomed that when the First Battle Group of the 19th Infantry returned to Augsburg in March 1962, he told me he had fallen head over heels in love with Berlin.

His face was rosy and wind-burned from the ten-hour ride in an open jeep, part of the army convoy. He was beautiful. We embraced, and he said, "Let's get a European discharge from the army. After my tour of duty, let's live in Berlin for a year. I want to study voice at the Hochschule für Musik and maybe even begin my singing career."

I was sure it would be just a year, then back to the States, where I would make a home and where I would become a citizen and finally belong. After all, Charles wanted to sing in America and build a career there. Right? These were questions I didn't dare ask him. Despite my adventures in the world of the West, I was still a compliant little Asian woman. I felt the strength of his arms around me. There, I was safe from my wanderings. The cold months of separation were over. The world was aglow with rainbows. My heart was a flutter. My husband was home. I would never be cold again.

"Okay," I said. "Let's."

CHAPTER 2

West Berlin

First, a small history lesson. During World War II, Germany invaded many European countries. Then Britain, France, and the United States, from the West, and Russia, from the East, fought to push Germany back to within the pre-1939 borders. After that the French, British, and U.S. forces divided up the western part of Germany and occupied it, and Russia occupied the eastern part. The city of Berlin was situated in that section of Germany occupied by Russia. The Western forces did not want this beautiful city to fall to the Russians exclusively, so Berlin was divided into four parts as well: the three parts on the western side going to the French, the British, and the Americans, and the eastern side going to the Russians.

Charles and I arrived in West Berlin in August 1962. The wall that cut through the city was one year old. Berliners called it the Wall of Shame. The city was utterly and totally consumed by the presence of the Wall and the events that its existence generated. Escapes from the eastern side of the city over the Wall and under the Wall and through the Wall happened daily and were ever more daring. Often escape attempts failed and the would-be escapees lost their lives: some were shot, some drowned trying to swim the canals. Sometimes the tunnels they dug collapsed on them. Only then would the escape route be reported in the papers to warn others to find another way. I absorbed all this but didn't quite know what to do with the knowledge. It just became a part of me.

Our immediate task was to find a home. One of the first German words we learned was *Zimmerfrei*, which means "rooms for rent." We stayed in a pension, and every day we read the *Zimmerfrei* columns in the morning papers, then headed out to the addresses listed. There seemed to be quite a few rooms for rent by someone named Immobilien. We traveled by bus, subway, or streetcar all over town, but after one week, we still had not located the right person to even show us a room. *Immobilien* was clearly not a word on the vocabulary list for army dependents learning German at the Army Education Center. (Weeks later we learned that *Immobilien* meant real estate agent. We should have gone there first if *Immobilien* was mentioned.)

One morning, as Charles was buying the paper at the corner kiosk, he saw on a notice board a familiar word: *Zimmerfrei.* He was writing down the address when a gray-haired woman tapped him on the shoulder. She pointed to herself and then at the card, explaining that the room was in her house. She was inviting us to come see it.

When she opened her front door that afternoon, the woman looked down at me and, as though I were not there, asked, "Is she a little Japanese lady?" Charles explained, "She comes from the Philippines." She added nothing to that statement, and I breathed a sigh of relief. She would not be asking any questions about the Philippines I could not answer.

The room was a large attic room with a dormer window looking out to a horse chestnut tree whose leaves were just beginning to gild at the edges. One couch, one bed, one cold water sink, one wardrobe, one hutch. The toilet was down the hall, and there was neither tub not shower. (We would learn to bathe in a basin.) The slanting ceiling made the room cosy and matched my romantic daydreams of carefree bohemians living the artists' life. Who needed the Puccini opera? Here it was. But I was a healthy Mimi, and I would not die.

For our first evening meal in our new home, we bought unwrapped, unsliced bread and inexpensive wine. We stood together, looking out of our dormer window at our tree.

I sighed and said, "Here, with a loaf of bread beneath the bough, a jug of wine, a book of verse . . ."

" . . . and a little piece of cheese," said Charles.

" . . . and thou beside me singing . . . Er, how does it go on?"

"Something about remolding the world."

Now that we had a Berlin residence, we had to travel about the city getting our new address properly registered at the local police station and then at the police department for foreigners. Each required document demanded two or three rubber stamps and signatures, and the stampers and signers were in offices scattered all over the city. A year after the building of the Wall, the city was still rearranging its offices and governmental departments. The German bureaucrats seemed impatient and angry, shouting their instructions to go to another office, not this one, for we often misunderstood directions. They seemed certain that the louder they shouted, the better we would understand. We crossed the city by bus, tram, and subway—one way of getting to know West Berlin.

One noontime our subway suddenly stopped. All subways throughout the western half of Berlin, all buses, all trams had halted for one minute of memorial silence. A few days before, East German border guards had shot an eighteen-year-old East German named Peter Fechter as he was attempting to scale the Wall and scramble to freedom. In plain view of people in the East and in the West, he was left screaming in agony for fifty minutes, until he finally bled to death.

For weeks afterward, West Berliners gathered in angry crowds along the Wall, holding up signs and shrieking "Murderers!" Peter Fechter was rocketed into martyrdom. Newspapers wrote dramatic headlines, and journalists filed moving stories about a city in torment. Relatives, friends, and former neighbors in the East were trapped in a headlock by a totalitarian regime. West Berliners looked across the barrier and knew they could not help, but they would not abandon family and friends. They would stay right next door, nearby.

Charles and I were caught up in the city's excitement and indignation. We, too, became infused with energy and purpose. Not that we ever actually did anything or said anything directly to anyone, not even Tante Susi or Onkel Werner, but there was a pervasive feeling of hurt in the air. Unjust things were happening in our midst. The city of Berlin defined a right and defined a wrong. God, it was great to be alive. It was exhilarating to be part of such an exciting city.

While West Berliners boycotted the S-Bahn (the East Berlin administered city train system) and paraded in demonstrations cursing the Wall, we went to see Onkel Werner about a job for Charles. Onkel Werner worked at the City Employment Office at Haendel Platz.

Mama and Papa back in Augsburg, always spoke German slowly, carefully, and with many gestures to help us understand them. But our Onkel Werner was a merry urbanite and quick of speech. He said, "Na, Charlie! Woll'n wa ma' seh'n wat wa kriegen! Wir werden kriegen wat wa kriegen können!"

Swiftly he pulled together the papers needed for Charles's employment. We sat in his office, admiring his efficiency, hardly able to utter a word. "Dankeschön" is all we could manage. When we emerged from his office, our heads were spinning from the strain of trying to decipher his words.

"I didn't understand any of that, did you?" I asked Charles.

"Not really. But he always said 'Krieg.' He was always talking about the war," said Charles.

I nodded. That much, I, too, had understood, or thought I had.

Later, when our German was becoming more fluent, we learned that *kriegen* is the German vernacular for the verb *to get*. Onkel had simply said, "Well, Charlie, we'll get what we can get." I still had much to learn, but the process of acquiring this new language, however painful, would do much to deepen my understanding of this new country.

The following week, Charles began working in a wholesale outlet that supplied plastic flowers, dolls, and teddy bear prizes at carnival grounds for games of chance and skill. His job was to pack large boxes with orders, such as fifteen teddy bears, sixty plastic flowers, and twenty dolls. None of this had anything to do with war.

It may be hard to picture West Berlin without its Europa Center, its I-Punkt rising above the city, and Breitscheid Platz in the visceral center of the former West Berlin abuzz with crowds and speakers, hawkers and roving musicians. But in 1962 the Europa Center had not yet been constructed, and the space beside the Kaiser Wilhelm Memorial Church provided ample room for carnivals and fun fairs. The lights of the tall Ferris wheels twirled into the night sky, and barkers at booths enticed the public to take a chance, buy a lottery ticket, try their skill at throwing darts or shooting moving targets.

Some weekends we would be drawn to the gaudy brightness, the loud music, the crowds, and the hurly-burly of the carnivals, and we'd see on display the prizes that Charles had so carefully packed into boxes during the week.

Soon after he had begun his new job, Charles announced, "We've been invited for coffee next Sunday at Hans's house."

"Who's Hans?" I asked.

"He's a nice little guy at work."

"Married?"

"I think so," said Charles.

Hans and his wife, Claudia, greeted us with great formality at the front door of their tiny apartment. The coffee table in front of the living-room sofa was set with a lightly starched tablecloth of pristine white and small, white embroidered napkins. The cups, saucers, plates, coffeepot, sugar bowl, and creamer were of fine china. The finery of that coffee table struck me as remarkable for there was nothing else in the cramped one-room apartment that echoed luxury. Clearly there was something important about this coffee time on a Sunday afternoon.

We were shown our places on the sofa, and soon steaming coffee had been poured into beautiful cups and a tall chocolate torte was served.

Claudia was a large, robust woman who towered over Hans. Hans was much older than I expected, and he moved about their small living space with slow deliberation, his strange black leather-gloved left hand hanging immobile at his side. Often in the years ahead I would see men with wooden hands gloved in black leather and understand that they were wounded veterans of the last war.

After Charles stopped work at the packing firm, we never saw Claudia and Hans again. That Sunday afternoon would blend with the memories of hundreds and hundreds of such pleasant Sunday afternoons.

We knew by now that Charles's job had nothing to do with war, nothing whatsoever to do with *Krieg*. And yet, this mistaken meaning for the verb *to get* made me think of a classmate in German class back in Augsburg. He had invited me for a soda after class. He was a nice enough young man who reminded me of my college friends in Los Angeles. I did not think it proper to go with him for a soda, so we stood and talked for several minutes at the Army Education Center after class. He told me that he would be transferring to Vietnam the next week. I wished him luck and forgot about him until I saw his photo in the *Stars and Stripes* newspaper five months later. He had been killed in action.

Even as that distant war was escalating, the Cold War of which we were now a part and its complexities would soon grip our hearts and complicate our lives. And that other war, the one still so alive and unwell in the psyche of our divided city, hummed on and on, to be uncovered by us in unexpected ways. War does not end when the bullets cease to fly. War lives on until somehow a healing can be found.

It was my turn to find work. In 1962, the U.S. Army would not hire American citizens for civilian jobs, preferring to keep those positions available to local nationals and others called third nationals. My Philippine citizenship meant that I was a third national, and as I could type and speak English, I got a job at the Press Center of the U.S. Army's Information Division. "She talks American, and she sure can type real fast," I heard an enlisted man tell his sergeant.

When I announced that I qualified for the job because I was a third national, Charles took me in his arms and kissed me saying, "Gee, you're a bank."

My English was fluent, and no one doubted that I would soon learn German. My job was to type press releases in English and German and send them to foreign correspondents and to local newspapers, as well as to radio and TV stations. When there was not enough time to mail out the releases, we would have to read them over the telephone. Some of the first sentences I learned in German were *"Guten Tag, hier ist die amerikanische Pressestelle. Wir haben eine Mitteilung fuer Sie, und zwar . . ."* (Hello, this is the U.S. Press Center. We have a press release that states . . .) Then I would read the release. I was forced to form my words carefully. I was compelled to learn the language.

Most of the press releases announced the travel of military units from West Germany to West Berlin through East German territory. Reinforcing battle groups (later reorganized into battalions) were sent regularly from West Germany through East Germany to West Berlin. Every three months a battalion would be sent back to West Germany, and another assigned to replace it. The exchange of these units meant two-way traffic of U.S. Army vehicles along the East German autobahn and across two East-West German borders. East German border guards checked the units' paperwork and let them pass, or held them up, causing what was known then as "another Berlin incident." The aim of the whole exercise was to demonstrate that West Berlin was a viable city, and it provided grist for our newscopy mill.

I worked in an office with two desks, two teletype machines, and a mimeograph. My office mate was a German woman from Hamburg who stood six feet tall in her stocking feet and wore her hair in a beehive, adding even more inches to tower over me. And her name was also Ruth. The other civilian employees, all German women, at the Press Center could not abide having two Ruths so I was given the name Lee. They all agreed that the new name was appropriate since I was *Asiatin.* In California, we used to call ourselves Oriental. *Asiatin* sounded like Asian. Well, the Philippines was in Asia, but I didn't feel Asian. I felt like a wanderer, who now had to get her tongue around an interesting new language.

To Charles's and my delight, when he auditioned for the Hochschule für Musik in October, he was awarded a full-tuition scholarship plus a monthly allowance so that he would not have to work. All was going so smoothly for us that we were certain our choice of Berlin for our home was right, at least for one year. *Well, maybe two.*

I had no inkling then of how completely Berlin would become part of my life, how its people would win my heart and yet at times hold me in horrified fascination, how its recent past would defy my understanding, and how its destiny would intertwine with mine.

President Kennedy was coming! With happy anticipation, West Berlin was preparing for his state visit. The city was eager for an opportunity to forget its troubles, and Berliners were desperate for someone to tell them that the hardships they were enduring were worthwhile. Some had lost jobs quite simply because they could not get to work when the border was sealed. Husbands were separated from their wives. Mothers were separated from their children. A bride and groom waved tearfully to relatives across barbed wire on a day when the family should have been together. For one bright and beautiful day at least the city would be a place of celebration and great joy.

The U.S. Army Information Division braced itself for the flood of journalists from all over the world coming to Berlin to cover the story. The Press Office of West Berlin's municipal government, the Berlin Senat, and the U.S. Army Information Division established a Kennedy Visit Press Accreditation Office down the hall from the Press Center, and I was assigned to work there. My job was to check the credentials of all journalists wishing to cover the visit and issue press passes. A different press pass would be needed for each of the stopping points of the presidential visit. I would accompany the press, ready to supply a pass just in case an accredited journalist had lost his or hers.

June 26, 1963, was the day that President John F. Kennedy visited West Berlin, and a day that West Berliners would long remember with a tearful smile. The trees of the city were in full leaf, flowers had been planted to welcome the tanned young American president, and a feeling of carnival filled the air.

Col. Louis Breault, the U.S. Army information officer, called his staff into his office at 9 A.M. He did not sit behind his desk to address us; instead, we all stood in a circle, and he was *very* earnest.

"There were fist fights among the journalists in Bonn yesterday. There were not enough press passes for everyone. We have to be prepared for all kinds of trouble today. There is a planeload of journalists following Air Force One. No one on board has a press pass. Do you have any more, Ruth?"

"Yes, Sir," I gulped.

"Good," said the colonel. Then turning to the man beside me, Captain Bainbridge, he said, "Captain!"

"Sir?"

"See that she is protected."

"Yes, Sir."

This was going to be an unforgettable day, I was sure. I felt no fear. History was happening again. My eyes were wide, drinking it all in. Captain Bainbridge and I got into an army car and drove to Tegel Airport in the northern part of the city. In 1963, Tegel Airport was not much more than the military airport of the French Occupation Forces. Most commercial passenger planes still landed at Tempelhof Air Field in the American Sector. Not until the early 1980s, as jet plane travel increased, would Tegel airfield in the French Sector become the main West Berlin commercial airport.

On the morning of President Kennedy's visit, we saw crowds already gathering behind the barricades along Kurt Schumacherdamm, the route the president's car was to take. The sun still lingered behind a morning haze, but we could see that it was going to be a sunny day.

When those pressmen without passes arrived, I had ten frantic minutes of handing out passes. I was seated on a chair, the press passes, which were cardboard tags with strings, in a cardboard tray on my lap. Captain Bainbridge stood beside my chair. The president was to stop at the Brandenburg Gate, the Free University, and Schoeneberger Rathaus, the main town hall in the West. The eager journalists pressed close, calling out the passes they wanted, until the tray was empty. Then all was well with the journalists, and no one asked for my services for the rest of the day.

When President Kennedy arrived, Berlin went wild. I was assigned a seat in the fourth press bus of the long presidential entourage. President Kennedy was way up ahead, waving to the cheering crowds, flanked by West Berlin's governing mayor, Willy Brandt, and Chancellor Konrad Adenauer. We were all pelted with flowers and confetti, even as far back as the fourth press bus.

Berliners young and old whooped and hollered as we passed. Gray-haired ladies waved flags and threw confetti. Young men and old men cheered. Squealing children had been let out of school. Fulsome Frauleins in skimpy summer dresses waved and waved with vigor. Some women were even waving their babies.

In the press bus, someone called out, "Hey, Joe, did you get a load of those two?" A United Press cameraman was behind me. His camera was pointed out the window, but it was not running. He winked at me and grinned. "Crowds love it, when they think they are being filmed," he said.

The sun was shining. There was a brisk breeze. Berlin was in ecstasy.

At the main city hall, President Kennedy endeared himself to the entire population by declaring, *"Ich bin ein Berliner."* I was in the cool inside corridor of the town hall. I could hear his words and the roar of the crowd. Was I a Berliner, too? Well, I was certainly a part of all this and being drawn in more and more.

While all this hubbub was going on, my conscientious student husband was whipping angrily up and down the empty corridors of the Hochschule für Musik. All of his classes had been canceled for the day, and he was furious.

That evening, I had just returned to our attic home and had collapsed on the bed, exhausted by the excitement of the day, when Charles arrived, raging. "They canceled all my classes! And what for? Just because a president's in town for a few hours! Ridiculous!"

I lifted a weary eyelid. "He's *your* president, darling, not mine. You ought to be more loyal."

"I'm not disloyal. I like the man. But why should his state visit interfere with my classes?" I must have fallen asleep for I didn't hear any more.

The euphoria engendered by the Kennedy visit continued for weeks and months afterward. People ran around saying, "Ish bien ein Berr-r-rliner-r," rolling the *r*s around in their mouths like Americans. My coworkers in the Press Center carried on about how chic Kennedy was, and so young and handsome. It seemed to me that Kennedy could lead them to do anything, and they would not question him. I watched them stand about in twos and threes and flutter and gush. They would follow him. They would blindly follow. I felt a cold shudder about me that was a combination of foreboding and reflection. I thought of a recent past when cheering crowds worshiped, with unquestioning loyalty, another leader. My colleagues spoke only German to me, but there was no mistaking the zeal of their adoration. West Berlin had been given the lift it needed.

The exchange of U.S. battalions continued, the Press Center announcing the exchanges, the crossings at the checkpoints, and most important, any delays caused by East German authorities.

Autumn arrived in burnished reds and yellows, the spirits of the city remained high, and the chestnut tree outside our attic window became a golden warrior.

At 8:00 P.M. on November 22, we were in our little one-room home, listening to the evening music program on AFN. We were finishing supper when the music was interrupted by an announcement that President Kennedy had been shot and was seriously wounded. There was a short interlude of music, then another announcement that President Kennedy was dead.

We sat stunned. A few minutes later, our landlady knocked on our door, and when we opened it, she just stood there, weeping. She could not speak, and we didn't know the right German words to say. We went to her to console her, not yet knowing how we ourselves felt but amazed at her enormous grief.

West Berlin slid into an agony of sorrow. At the U.S. Press Center, the two teletype machines beside my desk would click away throughout the night and on into the next days, telling stories about grieving people in countries all over the world. And the citizens of West Berlin were certain that they were at the center of it all.

Three days later, Charles and I joined thousands of Berliners making their way from all points of the city through the November gloom and converging on the square in front of the Schoeneberger Rathaus. Extra buses ran that night to handle the crowds. Berliners gathered before the Rathaus just as they had on that sunny day in June. We found ourselves in the midst of them, and many were sobbing. This time, the air was chilly and damp. This time, handkerchiefs were used to wipe away tears, not to wave. This time, Berliners were paying tribute to a lost friend.

After the speeches, buses carrying people from the square were so crowded that we decided to walk a while in the direction of home. The moist and penetrating cold that we were destined to know so well enveloped us now. Charles wrapped one arm around me for warmth as we walked. The street lamps glowed bravely through the fine mist that now was drizzle, then mist again. And everywhere we looked, on every window sill of every street, candles were lit, thousands of candles, burning in the night—*in memoriam.*

These German people were practically worshiping a fallen American hero. Inwardly, I was weeping with them. But once more I was an outsider. I wasn't an American yet. I had succeeded in exchanging my blue diplomatic passport for a regular tan passport of the Republic of the Philippines, that country of which I knew virtually nothing. Someday, I'd carry an American passport, then I could be proud of America, my country. For the time being, I sat on the edge of America, awaiting entrance. For the time being, I was visiting the Divided City, observing events around me, observing but not belonging.

Berliners were just drying their eyes from the sadness of late November when the hardly hoped for happened: East Berlin authorities were opening the Wall! If West Berliners applied for a Wall pass, they could go over to visit relatives in the East in time for Christmas. No, they couldn't come over to see you in the West. Don't even ask. You know they can't come over to the West. But families now separated by the hated Wall could be together after all. It didn't matter how complicated the paperwork was, West Berliners were willing to do whatever was necessary.

We were happy for these people for whom the Christmas season, especially Christmas Eve, held such family importance. Of course, we were separated from our own families as well. My parents were still at the Philippine Embassy in Seoul and Charles's family was in the United States, but it was our choice right now to enjoy this temporary European adventure. In a year or two, we'd return to the States. My, the stories we would tell. Better drink it all in now.

Gratefully, West Berliners formed long, long lines at crude offices hastily set up for the issuance of Wall passes. The winter of 1963-64 was a harsh one. In freezing temperatures people waited in line for as long as fourteen hours while bureaucrats exercised their power, winding red tape round and round the longing hearts of West Berliners. Young people, hoping to see parents or grand-parents, husbands or wives, on the other side of the Wall, waited patiently in the snow while children shivered. Old people, yearning to see their children in the East, grew faint in the cold and sometimes collapsed. The Red Cross sent around teams of high school students with thermos flasks of hot coffee to warm people who refused to give up their place in line although they were chilled to the bone.

In a country enjoying a postwar prosperity that outdistanced all other West European nations, these scenes of freezing people in long lines recalled times of suffering and deprivation and war. I did not know those desperate times. I had known no war. I was but a visitor here, an observer of a melancholy drama. And dancing in the back of my mind was an outrageous little notion that West Berliners almost welcomed the hardship because Berliners didn't want their situation forgotten by the world. Berliners now lived with the constant presence of a Wall. Such scenes would keep the international wire services peppered with Berlin datelines and hold the story of the city's special plight before the world. Even worse than the wounds of separation was the problem that Berlin might lose its place on center stage and be forgotten.

The Wall affected the lives of Berliners in many ways. We became acquainted with a couple who, like us, were planning to live in Berlin just one year, maybe two. Manfred was a native Berliner who had emigrated to Australia and married an Australian named Mandy. They were now in Berlin so that Manfred, an interior decorator, could renovate his mother's apartment. Manfred's mother was one of those lucky Berliners whose apartment was only slightly damaged by the war. In 1963, her apartment building stood alone on Feurig Strasse in the Schoeneberg District while empty lots lay on either side where bombed-out buildings had been cleared away.

The work would take several months. While waiting for Manfred to complete his task, Mandy took a job as a waitress, serving at cocktail parties and dinners in the stately homes of high-ranking American officials—homes in the Dahlem District of the city that had once been occupied by high-ranking Nazi officers. And so, valuable real estate had changed hands in the aftermath of war, but the genteel lifestyle of the ruling class continued.

We often double dated with the Australians, going to movies and concerts, or visiting each other's homes. Many dinners for four were prepared on the electric hot plate that Tante Susi had lent us and served on the two army footlockers—pushed together and covered with a tablecloth—that formed our dining table. Mandy and Manfred reciprocated by inviting us over for coffee and cake served in his mother's large, high-ceilinged living room. The room was never warm and cozy, for the apartment with its outside walls exposed to the cold was difficult to heat. And Manfred's frugal mother was not overly generous when feeding coal to the tiled heating oven that stood majestically in a far corner of a room. Memories of postwar scarcities hung almost visibly in the air.

One Saturday, when Mandy and Manfred were visiting us in our attic apartment, Charles said, "We have two tickets for a production of Benjamin Britten's opera *A Midsummer Night's Dream* in East Berlin, but Ruth can't go with me."

"Why not?"

"I'm a Philippine citizen. My government has no diplomatic relations with East Germany. My passport is invalid for travel to or through any East German territory," I explained.

Charles said, "So I wondered if you or Mandy would like one ticket. I'm sorry I can't offer two tickets."

"I can't go over there," said Manfred. "I'm a Berliner. This is not Christmas time, and I wouldn't be visiting relatives. That's when I could get a special Wall pass. Besides, we have two tickets next Saturday to hear Teresa Berganza at the Hochschule für Musik."

"Crumbs, what a batty city," said Mandy.

Unconsciously, we were becoming creative and inventive, as all Berliners must—despite the Wall. Or, maybe, because of the Wall.

So at 8:00 P.M. on the following Saturday, a Berliner and a Filipina listened to Teresa Berganza interpret Strauss, Dvorak, and Villalobos at the Hochschule für Musik on Hardenbergstrasse in West Berlin. Meanwhile, not far away, on the other side of the Wall at the Komische Oper in East Berlin, their spouses, an Australian and an American, were watching director Walter Felsenstein's magical interpretation of Shakespeare's *A Midsummer Night's Dream.* In that play, a certain line in Act V caused more audience clamor than the Bard had originally intended. When Bottom said, "Thou wall, O wall, O sweet, O lovely wall," the audience roared, then booed and whistled.

We never told Manfred's mother about this odd exchange. It was hard enough for her to understand what was happening in her city.

Since we could not go to East Berlin together, Charles had little incentive to visit the East. The single compelling lure in those early student days was to buy music scores.

"I can get music scores much cheaper in East Berlin," said Charles.

"Oh," I said with disinterest. For me, East Berlin was off-limits and seemed so far away. West Berlin was our city, the playground we were still exploring.

Now and then on a Saturday afternoon, we would catch any double-decker bus and run to the front seat on the upper level and ride to the end of the line. Often, the last stop would be at the Wall. From our front row seat, we'd stare down into that other world, the forbidden East. The booby-trapped no-man's-land had not yet been created just behind the Wall on the East side, but buildings were abandoned, window panes broken, weeds were taking over, and rats were enjoying population growth. The sight of the other side always made me feel as though someone had placed a cold brick in my stomach, and I'd be glad when the bus conductor collected our fares again for the return ride home.

The East was the "other" side of the city. We were happy in the West, West Berlin our home, our honeymoon home. With our arms around each other in that perpetual hug of newlyweds, we watched the city slide by below us. We were too young, too in love, too happy to stop and analyze political complications. Our life in the West suited us just fine.

Our struggle, in those first Berlin years, concerned our paltry German rather than politics. Gesticulating with our hands and feet, we told Tante Susi and Onkel Werner our weekly adventures. Our accounts were met with smiles and sympathetic understanding. What kindness we received from our new Berlin family, what patience, for our early attempts at speaking their language must surely have been pathetic—to say nothing of downright hilarious.

"I want to buy a helicopter," I announced to Tante Susi one evening while we were in the kitchen preparing supper. Tante Susi looked at me with those kind eyes that permitted me to struggle and fail.

"Helicopter?"

"You know—to keep the house clean."

"Oh, Rutchen. Not helicopter [*Hubschrauber*]; you mean vacuum cleaner [*Staubsauger*]."

"*Ja, Staubsauger*. That's what I mean," I said. I did not take offense at the laughter that ensued. We were in Tante Susi's kitchen, and I felt safe.

I worried about the cold of winter more than any laughter at my fumbling attempts at German. I experienced the cold as pain. Three winters would pass before I finally learned to dress for warmth. I bought fur-lined boots and long johns. From September through April, I never left the house without first putting one or two layers of sweaters on under my coat, then wrapping up in scarves and pulling on gloves.

Tante Susi had a special place for me in her living room. It was next to the handsome green-tiled coal heating oven in the corner. A little shelf set within the oven wall and enclosed by a hinged grating could accommodate a teapot or coffeepot and keep it warm.

Whenever we visited Tante Susi and Onkel Werner's apartment in the district of Lichterfelde, which was almost every Sunday afternoon, Tante Susi would first lead me to my special corner. Slowly, as the warmth of indoors seeped into my limbs, I'd remove the layers of outer clothing, rub my hands together, and begin to relax.

On Sunday afternoons we drank strong coffee and ate freshly baked cakes, while a large oil portrait of young Robert Schumann at the pianoforte smiled down upon us and on the table before us that was so festively set. Always in the early 1960s, Tante Susi would bake two kinds of cakes for Sunday afternoon coffee. And we would eat our fill. How welcome we felt. Sometimes Mama called from Augsburg, and we'd call out our greetings to her.

We would stay for a light supper of a wide selection of cold cuts, cheese, and condiments to make open-face sandwiches on our choice of whole grain dark breads—pumpernickel, Graubrot, or Brötchen. Always, there was so much to eat. When we prepared to leave, Tante Susi would remember to place my hat and gloves in the oven shelf for a few minutes to warm them. Then, after fortifying ourselves with a jigger of schnapps, we'd reenter the frigid outside, walk two blocks to the beautiful oak-tree-lined boulevard, Unter den Eichen, and catch the 48A bus to our attic home on Düeppelstrasse in Zehlendorf.

In our early years before our own children were born, it went without saying that the night before Christmas, *Heiligabend,* would be spent with our new Berlin family. On Christmas Eve we arrived in time for a late coffee that was singularly sparse, plain cookies replacing the rich homemade cakes of other afternoons.

At 6:00 P.M., when the winter night had settled in completely and a mist had formed on the insides of the windows despite the heavy blankets hung carefully between the double panes, Onkel and Tante excused themselves from the dining-room table, leaving their ten-year-old son, Christian, Charles, and me to wait in silence for *Bescherung,* the exchanging of gifts.

Then, at last, Tante Susi rang a bell and beckoned us into the living room while Onkel, his eyes all a twinkle, sat beside the heating oven, strumming on a guitar and singing, "*Ihr Kinderlein kommet* . . ."

We were allowed into the living room and the enchantment of Christmas Eve. The room was lit entirely by candlelight. The Christmas tree, adorned by lighted candles, stood fifteen feet high and was crowned by the smiling head of an angel. On every branch of the magnificent tree, silver tinsel hung, each strand equal in length, each strand having been placed there carefully by Tante Susi. On the floor beneath the tree was a manger scene of carved wood. The advent wreath, all four candles shining, hung from the center of the ceiling. In every corner of the room, a quartet of candles powered a miniature carousel. Tiny wood figures, fawns and lambs, kings and shepherds spun around sedately in flickering silence.

The room smelled of pine needles and cinnamon cookies, candle wax and goodness. Christian, Charles, and I were each directed to a *Bunte Teller*, a brightly colored plate filled with chocolates, cookies, fruits, and nuts. Beside the plate was a present.

Before opening our presents, we sang Christmas carols. Some of them were familiar, except for the German words. The parts we knew, we sang out with gusto.

"*O TANNENBAUM, O TANNENBAUM (wie schön sind deine Blätter. Du grünst nicht nur zur Sommerzeit, auch im Winter wenn es schneit.) O TANNENBAUM, O TANNENBAUM* . . ."

Christian then recited a Christmas poem, and Tante Susi and Onkel Werner told us of Christmases in the late 1940s, when food, clothing, and heating fuel were scarce. And we heard stories, too, about an even earlier time when Tante and Onkel's world was as innocent and carefree as ours. When Tante Susi read from the Bible, we knew the story well. We could understand the meaning of every word, even though it was all in German.

"*Fürchtet Euch nicht! Siehe, ich verkündige Euch grosse Freude* . . ." ("Fear not, for behold I bring you good tidings of great joy . . .")

I treasured these Christmas celebrations. I took note of every detail. Next Christmas or the year after, wherever we would be——

in the States, in the States, of course——I would try my best to bring the beauty of this evening to my own home.

I had been at the Press Center a year and a half when I began to write poems and short stories in the evening after work. Now and then I'd send off a manuscript. The first piece I ever sold was a filler about the plague of rats abounding in that strip of no-man's-land on the eastern side of the Wall. A pest-control magazine bought the filler for one dollar. The poems were for Charles and myself. They commemorated every passing month of our marriage, every birthday, every Christmas.

While I was experimenting with words, Charles was cast in a small role in Jacques Offenbach's *Die Banditen,* which was performed at the Freilicht Bühne Rehberger, West Berlin's outdoor theater. The show's two leading men were Fritz Hoppe and Helge Roswaenger: the first, the revered old gentleman of the Berlin stage; the second an internationally known tenor from Denmark.

The summer of 1964 was mild, the night skies clear, and productions in the open-air theater that year ran smoothly, even though the dialog was occasionally drowned out by the noise of a plane overhead. I did not understand yet that such interruptions were not viewed as an inconvenience, but rather as reminders that the city was linked at all times by air corridors to West Germany and its provisional capital, Bonn.

This was a particularly important reminder because Berlin's Wall was becoming more elaborate. Buildings in the East Sector just behind the Wall were being razed. Cinder blocks and barbed wire were replaced by smooth slabs of reinforced concrete, behind which now extended minefields guarded by dogs and studded by watchtowers. The Wall——that temporary horror, that momentary outrage—was acquiring an awful permanence.

This walled city was my home, but not forever, I thought. True, our little Berlin adventure was reaching into its third year, but it was still fascinating. We'd stay a little longer.

The horse chestnut tree outside our window unfailingly announced the passing seasons. As the golden leaves of autumn fell,
the soft spiky fruit fell, too, liberating the chestnuts within. In
winter, hoarfrost covered the tree's bare branches, and in springtime, blossoms unfolded in pink silence, later to drift downward,
laying a delicate mosaic upon the cobblestones beneath. Still later,
the early rains of summer came to wash the prettiness away.

Twice the cycle of seasons came and went, and we were very
happy. But by 1964, when the leaves of our tree had begun to gild
once more, we felt a restless stirring inside us.

"I have to have a piano," said Charles one day.

"I know how you feel," I said. "I want to have a baby."

We were outgrowing our cozy little place.

A rooms-for-rent card on the notice board at the Hochschule
für Musik advertised two rooms in a large apartment on Kaiser
Friedrich Strasse in the Charlottenburg District of town. The bathroom, kitchen, living room, and piano were to be shared with a
Finnish couple.

Kaiser Friedrich Strasse today presents a solid front of apartment building façades. Modern line architecture is sandwiched
between turn-of-the-century friezes. But in 1964, evidence of wartime devastation was everywhere. Buildings were still defaced by
the pockmarks of mortar fire, and gaping spaces showed where
buildings had been bombed away. Now and then a windowless
abandoned shell of architecture stared out at you, scarred by bullets and unseeing as a skull.

On the corner of Kaiser Friedrich Strasse and Spandauerdamm,
an empty space yawned in disinterest, allowing the wintry winds
that whipped across from the Charlottenburg castle to speed down
the street as though they were in a wind tunnel.(Later, we enjoyed
telling friends, "You know the Charlottenburg castle, where the
Princess Sophie Charlotte used to live? Well, we're just up the
street from there.") The side wall of the building beside this space
was adorned by bathtub fixtures dangling absentmindedly from

the third-floor level; and you could see the ornate tiles along the wall where a bathroom once had been.

We went to see the apartment. The Finnish family occupied two large rooms; if we chose to move in, Charles and I would have one large room and a smaller one. We would all share the large twenty-five-by-twenty-five-foot living room, the huge kitchen, the bathroom, and, of course, the piano.

We took the apartment, having immediately liked it and the Finns, though we could only communicate with them in fractured German since they knew just a few words of English and our knowledge of Finnish was nil. Their nine-month-old daughter, Laura, crawled happily around the apartment, speaking in Baby English, Baby Finnish, and Baby German with whoever would listen.

Ilpo, the husband, was on a scholarship to study with flutist Aurele Nicolet at the Hochschule für Musik. Pia, the wife, was also a flute player, but she was no longer performing. Her principle job was to look after Laura, their baby, and make sure absent-minded Ilpo remembered to take his music and instrument to the concert halls where he was engaged to perform.

I came home from the Press Center one evening to find Ilpo pointing a hair dryer at a pair of damp socks. Pia, eyes rolling heavenward, explained that they had forgotten he needed a clean pair for his performance that night.

Our new home was the meeting place for many of the foreign students at the Hochschule für Musik. Our parties were international gatherings. One student from Sweden named Lars played the flute and loved to recite Swedish poetry; a student from Istanbul sang a Turkish folksong, *Ushkidara,* and danced, clicking her fingers on top of her knuckles in rhythm. Maria was from Spain. Joachim was German. Dominique and Jean Pierre were French. At Christmas time, we sang *Silent Night* together, each in his or her own language. We had come from so many parts of the world and were now bound together by our love for music in this city of culture whose political life roiled and bubbled about us. We pursued our dreams with that special Berlin energy that smacked of derring-do, for the very air we breathed crackled with risk. We were, after all, in the middle of enemy territory. Once in a while, Charles would perform in a student recital at the Musik Hochscule, but most of the music making was impromptu fun in our own apartment. What an honor it was when Ilpo's flute teacher, Aurele Nicolet, attended one of our parties. The laughter and banter subsided a moment as the Maestro prepared to leave. "What fortunate young people you are," he said, "for you have music. No matter what happens to you later in life, you will always be rewarded because you have your art. Never let it leave you."

Our apartment was quietly thoughtful for several minutes after the Maestro left. Then our unfettered youthful energy reasserted itself, and the boisterous music making resumed.

"Do you know Schubert Lieder with *unanständige* words?" Ilpo asked the gathering. Ha-ha-ha. Naughty words. "Sing it, sing it," urged the guests.

Ilpo donned his fur hat and sat at the piano. Charles stood, fingers hooked at chest height, elbows out—and sang Schubert's *Erlkönig*. He ended not with the dramatic, " . . . *in seinem Armen, das Kind war tot*" (in his arms the child was dead), but with these words ". *in seinem Armen, das Kind hat gepinkelt*" (in his arms the child has peed).

After New Year celebrations ushered in 1965, winter marched on with a vengeance. Cold, snowy weeks stretched into months. I rose at seven every weekday morning and caught the yellow double-decker bus that carried me from the British Sector, where we lived, to the U.S. Press Center in the American Sector, where I worked. Berlin buses still permitted passengers to smoke on the upper level. Each morning and each evening I had the choice of being crushed by the rush-hour crowds downstairs or sitting in thick smoke upstairs. As often as possible, I ran upstairs to find a window seat, so

I could watch the city passing below and make believe that I was all alone and not in a crowded bus.

It had been four years now since the Berlin Wall had been erected. Because Charles's and my understanding of German had improved greatly, people began telling us the stories of how their lives had been disrupted by the Wall. The secretary who worked at the Public Affairs Office of the U.S. Mission, a few doors away from my office at the Press Center, told me that in August 1961, she had returned from a vacation in West Germany to discover that the Wall stood between her workplace in West Berlin and her home in East Berlin. Later, she and thousands of Berlin citizens like her would have to choose between their jobs on one side or their homes on the other. Fearing reprisals from the East German regime because she worked for the Americans, she chose to stay in the West. It was not an easy decision because she still lived at home with her parents.

While ordinary citizens had had to choose between East and West, extraordinary citizens such as the renowned East German theater director Walter Felsenstein continued to work at the Komische Oper in East Berlin, crossing the border after work to return each evening to his comfortable villa on Mexiko Platz in West Berlin. He was so respected by East German authorities and his work in East Berlin so valued that the Wall could not stop him.

Although Felsenstein did not fear the East, others in West Berlin were not so calm. Sudden loud noises made people jump.

One day in spring 1965, I was on my way to the laundromat across the street when the air was split by a tremendous BOOM! I saw the window pane with the washing machines behind it shudder and bulge, even as I moved—slow motion—inside a world of sound. BOOM! I was within the boom. I became part of it. It stole my breath. Yet I kept moving, slowly, unable to comprehend that I'd been hammered by sound, invisible like the wind. The wind was in the dancing trees, pushing clouds across the sky. But this was sound. BOOM! There, engulfing you before you were aware that it had come. A shroud dropped on you, so now you were enveloped by sound. BOOM! BOOM!

Should you duck into a doorway to escape the sound? Could you run from the sound when nothing has moved but your throbbing eardrums? Did I really see that shop window pane shudder and bulge? The sound of shattering glass behind me told me yes. Sound was visible. The aftermath was visible. Fear should jab at your solar plexus and make you run and hide. What were you hiding from? Sound? Invisible sound? BOOM!

In the spring of 1965, Soviet MIG jets, flying low over the city, were breaking the sound barrier again and again, scaring West Berliners out of their wits. The sonic blasts resounded with memories of bombs and shelling. Was it any wonder that West Berliners were jittery? Some kept a suitcase packed at all times, just in case the Russians invaded.

Was I packed? Was I ready for the Russian invasion? The joke told again and again was that if the Russians did invade, the American GIs would not even have time to get their pants on. Ha-ha-ha! But still some friends whispered that they were packed.

What would I grab if the Russians invaded? A warm coat. If it were in the middle of summer, would I remember to grab the warm coat?

People may still have feared an invasion from the East, but "Berlin incidents" were becoming fewer. Reinforcing battalions still plied the stretch of autobahn between Helmstedt and Berlin, but East German harassment had become so infrequent that the U.S. Army had little opportunity to issue a statement of abhorrence. Finally, three and a half years after it had begun, the exchange of reinforcing battalions, a President Kennedy idea, ceased altogether. My job at the Press Center was groaning onward in humdrum routine.

I wrote a piece about an American artist and his rendition of the Wall in oil. A U.S. magazine bought the piece for $200.00, and I was so encouraged that in March of 1965, I resigned from the Press Center and declared myself a freelance writer and translator. Article sales for the next four years were a breathtaking annual event, but translation work was steady.

The only thing I missed about going to work was a circle of land called Innsbrucker Platz that I always looked for beyond my bus window. Innsbrucker Platz was a quiet space set in the middle of whizzing urban traffic, where the Schöneberg and Steglitz Districts met. The circle was dotted here and there by benches and shrubs, and etched straight down the middle by streetcar tracks.

In summer, this grassy haven baked in the sunshine, old people sat motionless on benches, and children fed the cheeky sparrows and pigeons, while the merry-go-round of traffic sped around them. In winter, the grassy disk was covered with snow, which remained clean and white while the rest of the city's snow was soon besmirched by urban filth.

But Innsbrucker Platz was most important as springtime approached. Every year, before they appeared anywhere else in the city, crocuses, daring the calendar, sprang up on Innsbrucker Platz, thanks to the subway line running beneath it, sending up waves of warmth long before the welcome air of spring. When the winter months dragged on and weary commuters began to wonder whether spring would ever come—then purple, blue, and white crocuses would thrust through the snow at Innsbrucker Platz. And when the flowers appeared, I could feel the silent sighs of my fellow passengers and sense a slowing of the traffic flow. For we had seen the crocuses, and our spirits had been renewed.

Wherever Charles and I would live in the future, after we had said good-bye to this temporary stopover, I'd be sure to remember this spot, this Innsbrucker Platz, and its message of springtime renewal. I promised myself that, years hence, as an old woman, I would revisit Innsbrucker Platz because it had taught me about hope when I was still young.

In summer 1965, I was translating magazine and newspaper articles from German into English for a British journalist. I would sit for hours at my manual Smith Corona typewriter, picking my

way through German internesting clauses, then reweaving them
with English syntax. Meanwhile the little baby inside me was growing and kicking more and more vigorously in protest as the noise
of typing passed through the amniotic fluid to delicate, forming
ears. To quiet the active child, I stuffed a pillow between my pro-
truding middle and my Smith Corona—and continued to work.

As I typed, I kept our little transistor radio tuned to AFN, our
link to the country across the ocean to which I yearned to return.
While our first offspring stamped energetically on my bladder, I
listened to sirens and explosions, the crashing of glass, and hoarse
angry voices.

"Burn, baby, burn!" The Watts District of Los Angeles was on
fire.

I lifted my fingers from the keys and listened. And the child
within me stopped dancing and seemed to listen, too. The very
typewriter on which I was working I had bought from the White
Front store on Central Avenue, not far from Watts. I began to
think about the future. To which world would our half-black, half-
Asian child belong? Would this child be colored or Negro or black?
(African-American hadn't come into usage yet.) Could I give this
child anything from the Philippine culture, when I seemed to
have lost it in my search for adventure? Would the broken glass
and ashes of Watts signal the breaking down of barriers and walls?
After the fire was over and the evidence of anger swept away, would
we have a better world in which my child could grow and be
happy? Or would there be a great division of peoples' hearts and
minds, like the Wall in Berlin?

As I pondered this, I heard Charles practicing in the next room.
He was preparing for an audition. One week before, I had taken a
phone call from a casting director.

"We need someone to play Freddie in *My Fair Lady*," said the
agent.

"But . . . but," I stammered. "But Charles is a . . . a baritone."

"Yes, but we've heard he has a good high range."

"That's true," I said. I didn't want to describe Charles further and wrote down the time and place of the audition.

"*My Fair Lady?*" said Charles when he came home that evening. "*Fair* Lady?"

"He said he'd heard you had a good high range." Charles was silent.

When the show's producer and Charles met, they both had to agree that Charles was not quite the right person to play Freddie. On suggesting Charles for the role, the agent had only mentioned the quality of his voice not the shade of his skin.

Several months later, on a snowy morning in late December, Charles and I were both cast in new roles—no auditions required. The day was December 27, traditionally the German housewife's holiday. The diligent German housewife, who has baked, cooked, cleaned, and shopped for weeks before Christmas, is finally allowed a day of rest. Not so secretly, everyone else wants to take a day of rest as well.

Unfortunately, our soon-to-be first-born child had her own ideas. My contractions were fifteen minutes apart by the time we arrived at Rittberg Krankenhaus in the district of Lichterfelde. A skeleton staff was on duty, and they were openly miffed because they had to work on a day that should be a national holiday. Germany had closed down as of noon on December 24. December 25 and 26 were already official holidays, but the Germans wanted more.

Charles was sent home by a disgruntled hospital employee with a wave of the hand. "No use you staying here; this is going to take a long time." I was left alone in a room for the first nine hours as my labor progressed. No one offered painkillers, comfort, or even encouragement. I could hear conversations about me in the corridor outside the open door. If I would only cooperate and produce this baby, why, they'd all have a much easier time of it. Although I understood every word they spoke, I was too occupied with my own work, too alone, and too scared to formulate a good German sentence. I kept my eyes on the single naked lightbulb hanging overhead and on the wall clock. Twelve hours had elapsed since I had been brought into this room.

When it finally came time to push, I was quickly wheeled into the delivery room. The midwife's fury was directed at me. She scolded and slapped my splayed thighs. "What is the matter with you, can't you even produce this one child? Look at me, I've had three boys." Slap. Slap. Slap. A pinch on the thigh again and again will hasten this slow foreigner who is clearly not trying hard enough.

Germans are incredibly direct and to the point. "It's a girl. Pretty." Through my exhaustion, I asked weakly to see her, but I was told no, not yet, she had to be bathed first. Our daughter was whisked away and wasn't brought to me until the next afternoon, a little white bundle swaddled tightly, her thick long black hair conspicuous amid the surrounding baldness of German babyhood.

When Charles came to see me, I wept in his arms. "They were so mean to me."

"You will never have to have another baby in Germany," he promised. Good, I thought, that means we will soon leave this dreadful place.

You can't generalize about Germans any more than about other people. The cruel midwife and the grumpy salespeople were all Germans. But so were Onkel Werner and Tante Susi, who were always ready with calm assistance and advice for new parents.

Adored as "*die süsse, kleine Schwarze*" (the sweet little black child), our daughter, Lynne, was fussed over by women we met on the street who reached into their purses and pulled out bonbons, pressing them into Lynne's hand or sometimes (because it's more sanitary) merrily unwrapping a piece of candy and poking it directly into her mouth. Horrified, I would glare at these women who were only trying to show kindness the best way they knew how and who shook their heads at the unwarranted rudeness of this foreign mother. A good German mother would have smiled sweetly and thanked them.

One afternoon, seven months after Lynne's birth, two men strode importantly into the apartment. They were measuring walls and windows, inspecting plumbing fixtures, and counting electrical outlets. One man was the apartment owner, the other was a prospective buyer. It would cost DM 5,000 to renovate the apartment; if we could not come up with the money, we would have to move out when the rental contract with the Finns lapsed next month. Ilpo had finished his studies, and he and his family were returning to Finland. Charles, Lynne, and I had to look for a new home.

CHAPTER 3

Nollendorf Platz

On Motz Strasse near Nollendorf Platz, we found a one-bedroom apartment with a large living room–dining room and a small room that would be perfect for the nursery. The place made you tilt your head and squint, as if the architect had been a bit tipsy when he designed it. A closer look revealed an absence of right angles wherever two walls met. Had the architect never heard of the perpendicular? The building had once accommodated large sprawling apartments, like our apartment on Kaiser Friedrich Strasse, but the advent of the Berlin Wall had depressed property values and a shrewd West German businessman had bought the building and divided it into several smaller units. In each, he had installed central heating and a tiled bathroom. All walls were painted white, but the workmanship was slapdash, the floors so hastily covered with linoleum that the glue was still oozing from uneven seams. Each smaller apartment was rented for twice the price of the entire undivided one we had had.

An unfurnished apartment in Berlin was precisely that. There was a sink and an electric stove, but nothing else in the kitchen. Bare wires poked out from the walls where we would later attach light fixtures. We brought with us from Kaiser Friedrich Strasse the few pieces of furniture we had acquired and one very important floor lamp.

For the first week in our new apartment, we were able to cultivate a wonderful family togetherness, for after darkness fell, we moved about our little flat together, always together, unplugging and plugging in our floor lamp, our only source of light.

Our living-room windows looked across the street to an empty apartment building whose windows were boarded shut. At night it stood like a looming black shadow against the city sky. Our bedroom and kitchen windows faced the back courtyard and the building's rear wing.

We never met the apartment-house owner. All questions or complaints were handled by our concierge, Frau Meister, who was jolly and fat and often toothless, for her dentures were either in her mouth or not, according to no set pattern that I could tell. She made no apologies for the loose bun that would slide down the back of her head and remain in a state of imminent undoing.

Frau Meister lived with her daughter and baby granddaughter. We often heard sounds of laughter or scolding coming from the apartment beyond the courtyard, where the three generations of Berlin women lived.

Sometimes, in the entranceway of our home on Motz Strasse, we would meet an American soldier on his way to the back courtyard. We always exchanged a friendly, "Hi! How're ya doin'?"

One evening I answered a knock at our door. I had Lynne straddling my hip when I opened the door. A baby on her own hip, Frau Meister's daughter stood outside. She wore her hair in a blond beehive, and her blue eyes were set a bit too closely together. My straight black hair fell past my shoulder blades. We mothers could not have been more different, but our daughters might have been mistaken for cousins, with large sparkling brown eyes and black curly hair. Frau Meister's daughter asked if she could use our phone and if I could please dial for her and ask for Sgt. Robinson, as her English was not very good.

We went to the phone in the bedroom. I could tell by the answering voice that I had dialed a U.S. Army barracks number. When the sergeant came to the phone I wanted to give my neighbor some privacy, but when I left the bedroom, the two babies complained tearfully. And putting the baby girls together in Lynne's playpen led to howls of protest. There was nothing for it but to remain in the bedroom. I could tell that the sergeant was returning soon to the United States, which made the young mother weep and complain.

As summer progressed, Frau Meister's daughter became heavier and moved more slowly, and in September, another baby daughter joined the family of women in the apartment beyond the courtyard.

Friendships, first formed during my days at the U.S. Press Center, remained true, and we were often invited to parties across town in the Dahlem District, where members of the American Foreign Service lived in huge homes. At these parties, we met U.S. news correspondents who had known Berlin long before the Wall was built. They spoke of a united city we could hardly imagine.

If you mark the 1948 Berlin Airlift as the beginning of the Cold War, then that war was now eighteen years old. There seemed to be no satisfactory resolution to this nonshooting war in sight. The city of Berlin was slipping in newsworthiness, and the number of foreign correspondents in the city was dwindling.

"What we need is a war, another war," complained a veteran United Press correspondent. "Then, they'd really want us here again."

The announced retirement and return to the United States of veteran news correspondents Edgar and Katharine Clarke of the *Washington Post* resulted in a flurry of cocktail parties to bid them farewell. Once more Charles and I—although we were not with the U.S. Mission, the U.S. Army, or the U.S. press corps—were somehow included on the invitation list.

Throughout the summer of 1966, we went to one cocktail party after another. Drinks and dainty canapés were served by waitresses in short black dresses and white aprons, reminding me how much I missed Mandy, who had returned with Manfred to Australia.

At first the parties we attended were in honor of the departing Clarkes; later, the parties celebrated other events. Always we brought along our baby, whose only nourishment was mother's milk— probably the richest food in town.

Students at the Hochschule für Musik came back from the 1967 Easter break to find Charles no longer there. He was now studying privately with Professor Ernst Garay.

"He's really a wonderful teacher, Ruth," said Charles after a lesson one day.

"I'm glad."

"He has those tattooed numbers on his arm, you know."

A shiver of horror ran down my back. So he'd survived a concentration camp. Professor Garay had obviously seen terrible things in the sixty-some years of his life. A tenor in his day, he still led services as cantor and enjoyed a reputation as a fine voice teacher. Charles was taking lessons daily, determined to secure a solid vocal technique and build a career. As the two worked together, the magical bond, connecting wise counselor/teacher and eager student, danced in that glowing space of energy between them. Garay was like a father to Charles, who called him Papa.

Charles was dashing into the elevator one afternoon, running late for his lesson with Professor Garay. The metal doors of the elevator clanged shut and as he stood, catching his breath, he saw scratched into the gray paint: "*Jude—'raus aus Deutschland!*" (Jews— get out of Germany!) Anger filled his chest and sent icy fingers up into his throat.

Minutes later, in Professor Garay's apartment, the warm-up exercises went poorly. The professor told Charles to do them again. And again. "What's wrong? What's wrong with you today?"

Outrage dissolved into choking sobs. Charles managed to gasp, "Elevator . . . elevator."

Garay knew what Charles meant. He, too, had read the dreadful words. Not pausing for a moment, Garay scolded, "Stop that now! We have a lot of work to do. We do not have time for such things. People who do that are nothing but idiots. Now breathe. Let's do that exercise again."

Charles worked hard at his lessons and hard to support his little family. He took a myriad of small jobs: church solos, the baritone part in local performances of cantatas and oratorios. We had a little plastic container, shaped like a mushroom, where we kept money. The mushroom's red lid sported white dots. (These *Fliegenpilze,* or toadstools, are a symbol of good luck in Germany.) Charles ran to rehearsals and performances and lessons; and into the little red mushroom, he put his earnings. Often, I'd remove the last twenty-mark bill to buy groceries. Always another small engagement would come through, and we'd have enough money for our needs.

While Charles was earning money, my job was to look after our daughter. Playgrounds in Berlin are like giant sandboxes. When children land on the ground after a slide down the slide or a jump from a swing or a fall off the jungle gym, they land on deep soft sand. Often these playgrounds are at intersections of two or more streets, places where bombs in the Second World War had hit their mark and blocked traffic in several directions at once. Now these intersections are playgrounds.

How innocently we pursued our dreams. Charles was, gig by gig, building a career. I was cooking, shopping, helping a toddler into little clothes. Sometimes in the afternoon after her nap, I'd dress Lynne in play clothes and head for the playground on Viktoria Luise Platz. Not far from this peaceful playground, protesters often battled with police. Friends in the United States read newspaper accounts of the trouble in our divided city and wrote letters of concern. From across the sea, I learned of a riot that had taken place a few blocks away from where Lynne filled her bucket full of sand then emptied it, laughing, on to her shoes.

The war in Vietnam was stirring up the protest-loving Berliners again. Demonstrators scrawled the words "*Ami* [Americans] Go Home" on the walls of the American-financed Henry Ford

Building at Berlin's Free University. Ironically, the right and free-dom to protest at all depended on American presence in West Berlin, not absence. Marchers protested against the university sys-tem that the rioters claimed was unfair to students. Rioters clashed often with police in a mélange of banners and billy clubs, antiwar chants and water cannons. When the shah of Iran visited West Berlin, protesters took to the streets yet again.

More ominous were the Russian tanks that rolled into Czechoslovakia's capital on the evening of August 20, 1968. In a bid to free themselves from Soviet rule, Czechs in Prague were mounting a revolution. West Berlin held its breath in fearful an-ticipation of what might happen. Our friend Joachim telephoned. Had we heard the terrible news? Prague was being invaded. So what? I thought, not knowing that the beleaguered city was not even 200 miles away from where we lived.

Prague, Czechoslovakia, and indeed the entire Eastern Bloc were almost mythical places to my uninformed mind. Since I couldn't travel to any Eastern Bloc country, they sort of didn't exist. I always flew in and out of West Berlin. It truly was as though I were living on an island.

On television that night, we saw people throwing rocks at tanks.The next day, I put Lynne into her stroller and went shop-ping. There was not one single sack of potatoes in the supermar-ket, nor in the next three grocery stores. All shelves were cleared of staples such as flour, sugar, and salt as well. I couldn't believe my eyes. What had happened to all the food?

The Berliners, remembering the days of the 1948-49 Block-ade, remembering the scarcities of war, had stocked up. The doc-tors in the city had been told not to travel outside it. I was jolted into a renewed awareness of what our situation really was. I was being reminded that West Berlin was isolated deep inside East Germany, 110 miles behind the Iron Curtain. Somehow, in my rounds of caring for a toddler and a home, I had forgotten.

Yet even as protesters battled the police and Russia invaded Prague, West Berlin was rebuilding itself. West Berlin, our city, our home, was changing all about us. War ruins were being blown up and cleared away, and modern apartment buildings were rising in the spaces left behind. Buses were replacing trolley cars, and new subway lines were under construction.

With Lynne beside me in her stroller, I stood on the corner of Martin Luther and Kleist Streets one day and looked across at a space once filled by war ruins and unkempt underbrush. Four building cranes stood in a row, like gigantic praying mantises, glinting in the sun. Behind me was a block of ruins overgrown now by weeds. And I knew that someday modern high-rises would stand in their place.

On turning homeward, Lynne and I were overtaken by two very tall women. One had huge red curls; the other wore a blond bouffant. The tall ones were strung with necklaces and bracelets and were heavily made up, their long false lashes thick with mascara.

"Oh, how adorable she is," said one woman, bending over Lynne. "Let the Tante give you a little gift." And she pressed into Lynne's small hand a ten-pfennig coin. They strode away, their high heels clicking on the pavement, their narrow hips wiggling provocatively. And as they turned the corner, I heard them laugh the deep-throated laughter of men.

Even though heating oil now warmed our home, careless management of it taught us we could not rely on its availability. Frau Meister's daughter, every hair of her blond beehive neatly in place, was at our door once more.

"We are so terribly sorry," she said, "but we are about to have no heat."

"What do you mean?" I said.

"Our heating tank has no more oil." Our apartment house owner lived in Hamburg, she explained. It was his responsibility to order the oil and keep the tank filled. But, oh, Frau Meister's daughter was so very sorry, now the tank was empty and she and her mother, despite many phone calls, even telegrams, were not able to contact him. He was away in the Canary Islands on vacation. She was terribly sorry about it all.

It was January 1969, and temperatures hovered around twenty degrees Fahrenheit. We, too, would soon be terribly sorry about it all.

Well, at least we still had electricity. We turned on all three hot plates and kept the oven on. We stayed in the kitchen or huddled together in bed, or best of all, we spent long hours visiting friends in their warm apartments.

After one week, the building owner returned from vacation, and we had heat in the apartment once more. It had only been a week, but I realized that the enemy "cold" could make a reappearance anytime.

One afternoon in spring, I opened the apartment door to an insistent ring. Frau Meister herself filled the doorway, smiling at me with no teeth. I had just discovered the 19th-century Berlin cartoonist Heinrich Zille and was charmed by his drawings. Now, here was a Zille figure in colorful reality. She was wearing thick felt slippers and heavy socks. Her hair was in its perpetual state of dishevelment, and she was announcing some important news.

We were not to worry, but there would be an explosion at 11:00 A.M. the next day. They were blowing up the empty building across the street. We were to stay indoors and keep all the windows shut tight.

At the appointed hour, I took Lynne into my arms, and Charles and I stood at the living-room window. Traffic on the street below had been diverted, so all was still. Then a thud and a rumble filled the air while a thousand cracks ran like rivers on the building's face. The soft percussive thud seemed distant yet coming somehow from all directions. The building across the street sagged and trembled, then, in mesmerizing slowness, it collapsed. And from the pavement gray clouds billowed upward so thickly that the world was soon engulfed in a gray and eerie light. Lynne whimpered. I held her close but could not take my eyes away from the crumbling scene before us.

We breathed shallowly, trying not to inhale the dust that already was filling the space between the double-paned windows, trying not to let the dust into our lungs. But we had to breathe and continue our day, of course, and we had to clear away the dust that had so quickly settled on every surface.

Later I took a rag and a broom and attacked the dust that had crept into all the rooms. I swept and dusted for the rest of that day, into the next week, and on into the months and even years that followed. But still I would find dust in corners, deep cracks, and other hidden places. For the dust of a war where shooting had ceased decades before would not be swept away so easily in a city where a peace treaty had yet to be signed.

So, as our city, our half city, our amputated metropolis, moved onward to the 1970s, we watched, transfixed, as if standing on the edge of a restless sea. I wanted to remember all of these events but feared they would cast a spell on me somehow and tie me to Berlin. I wanted to be ready to move at a moment's notice. I wanted to be in America where I wouldn't have to struggle with the cold and the language. Yet each event in this city fascinated us. Each happening washed over us like a wave. And with each wave we sank deeper and deeper into the sandy soil of Brandenburg.

Twice in the three winters we spent at the Motz Strasse apartment, the central heating broke down. Twice freezing temperatures drove us out of our apartment for up to a week. By 1969, we were determined not to face another winter without heat, so it was important to find a home where we could control the heating-fuel supply ourselves.

Lilli Sommerfeld, a member of the Johannische Church, heard that we were apartment hunting and invited us over to her home for a drink. She was alone in the world now, she explained, and although she had intended to see out her days in the Halensee apartment, where she had been born sixty years before, she now realized that it was far too big a place for her.

We asked how the apartment was heated. She showed us the coal furnace in the kitchen. "See? All you have to do is stoke the fire like this." She crouched before the furnace and pushed beneath the coals the long steel stoker that ended in an oval handle. A small puff of coal dust rose from the sounds of scraping and the drizzle of coal ash into the metal drawer below. "See how clean it is? No trouble at all."

The winter of 1969-70 was damp. The steel-gray February sky outside allowed little light to enter the kitchen. The belly of the furnace was half-filled with glowing coal, and in the kitchen with our coats still on, we were warm. We'd learn how to make this work for us, we promised ourselves. It's easy, Lilli kept reassuring us.

The coal furnace in the kitchen heated the radiators in each room. We would have our own supply of coal in the cellar two flights down, and it was up to us to keep the furnace sizzling and warm. "You are a nice young couple," she said, pouring three little glasses full of schnapps. "I would like us to drink to your new home." Charles and I looked at each other in disbelief. With the city's housing shortage so critical, we knew how lucky we were to be offered such an apartment. Hundreds of apartments stood empty, waiting for renovation, while city bureaucracy became stuck in underefficient or overefficient organization. Berliners, of course, protested with waving banners and parades, and often squatters took up illegal residence. We clinked schnapps glasses and downed the drink. It burned a bright, warm path down my esophagus and into my tummy and left me tingling with a sense of well being.

Lilli had some sway with the building owner as she and her family had owned the house before becoming renters themselves. She would persuade the present owner to permit us to move in.

In March 1970, we moved to the Halensee District of town. I noticed how much more there was to move this time. You need more furniture and more equipment when you have one baby and another on the way. Parental responsibility was dampening the blithe abandon of our child-free days. With a second baby due at the end of summer, I began to wonder how soon we'd be saying farewell to this new residence. It, like all the other addresses in my life, was temporary, I was sure.

As usual, the pressing minutiae of life prevented me from analyzing, philosophizing, and dissecting my thoughts. Conversations with friends were filled now with life's gritty practicalities, such as paying bills, which came regularly although income happened irregularly. I was learning about shoveling coal into two buckets, each of which could hold ten pounds of the fuel. I would carry the buckets from the coal cellar to our apartment two flights up. Tiny bicep muscles would gradually push outward on my upper arms.

Summer was looming ahead when suddenly there were no more singing engagements for Charles. The little elevator in my stomach was descending fast. Smile. Something will turn up. And it did. Berlin's city government provided its unemployed performing artists with work. Charles became part of a Berlin program called Kuenstler Dienst (Artists' Service). Paid a modest wage, Charles participated in a musical program of light entertainment. He had two solos and sang in the finale. The troupe of otherwise out-of-work performers traveled to school auditoriums, senior citizen centers, and hospitals to present their programs.

Between shows we were invited once more to a dinner party at the home of members of the American Foreign Service. Charles excused himself right after the first course, explaining that he had to slip away to sing in a program, but he would be right back.

"Oh, Jochen will drive you there, Charles," said our host.

So Charles rode in a chauffeur-driven car to a school auditorium on the other side of town. And after the program, the uniformed driver brought him back to the beautiful house on a tree-lined boulevard in Dahlem. Charles winked at me as he joined the after dinner conversations over coffee and cognac. And I winked back.

On a very hot July day in 1970, I sat in a straight back chair, my feet propped up, my enormous belly extending before me like a dear little coffee table. We were in the large sprawling apartment of friends on Clausewitz Strasse, and we were all watching the live television coverage of the final game of the World Cup in Mexico City.

Pele was the soccer star that year. Kneeling to cross himself before every free kick, he led his Brazilian team to a four-to-one victory over Italy. After each goal one of our friends, a young doctor, ran up and down the apartment's long hallway yelling, "*Tor! Tor! Tor!*" (Goal! Goal! Goal!), while our second offspring, waiting for his entrance, listened quietly.

For my second parturition, I had carefully chosen a hospital, Martin Luther Krankenhaus, where husbands were allowed in the delivery room. On August 24, 1970, our son, Scott, was born. His arrival was so precipitous that although the hospital was a mere four-minute drive from our apartment on Seesener Strasse, my water broke before we could reach the maternity wing, and our footsteps splashed and slid as we hurried to the labor room. (No, they don't put you in a wheelchair the moment you enter the hospital as in the United States.) This time, the midwife was gentle and kind and had hardly anything to do. This time, Charles stayed with me through the delivery and was even allowed to assist.

"He let me hold the scissors," said Charles, grinning.

This time, we and our new son were permitted to be together for a few quiet moments without the bustling hospital staff. Was it possible that Berliners' manners were mellowing? Or were we just more at home? Certainly, by now, our spoken German was fluent. Does fluency of language have something to do with acceptance?

I shared a hospital room with two other new mothers. Our babies were brought to us at regular mealtimes, and then they were whisked away until the next feeding.

A fourth bed was empty until a petite blond mother-to-be was wheeled in and placed upon it. Her water was leaking, poor thing, although contractions had not yet begun. She was frightened and would not stop talking. For twenty-four hours she talked and talked. As our babies were brought to suckle and burp and be taken away again, as our meals were brought and dishes cleared, the blond woman told her story over and over again.

Just two years before, when she was nineteen years old, she, her twenty-one-year-old brother, and her twenty-year-old fiancé had fled from the East. They had planned their escape carefully, withdrawing all cash from their savings accounts, and leaving the money in their rooms with farewell letters to their parents. Then they had set out with one long knife and nothing else but the clothes they wore. Across the minefield leading to the border, they crawled on their bellies; the fiancé first, she in the middle, her brother behind. Her fiancé carefully inserted the knife into the earth every six inches. If the blade met metal, they shifted to the left or right. If no metal was detected, they wriggled forward.

It would take them four hours to traverse the mined death strip between East and West. When they came to the barbed wire barrier, they removed their sweaters and draped them over the wire to protect their hands. Then they clambered over the barbed wire and dropped down into the West.

"We turned ourselves over to the police then," she said, crying a little. She would not tell us exactly where they had crossed, but we knew it was not in Berlin where all barbed wire fencing had been solidified into the Wall.

Her storytelling held us spellbound, and it seemed to stimulate her contractions. Soon she was taken away and returned four hours later with a son.

We mothers chatted now and then between the hospital's clockwork regime of meals and baths and visitors. We all shared this peculiar half-city with its special symbolism, its clear challenge, and its hope. We were all Berliners, we declared with pride. Even I, an ex-patriot without a homeland, was caught up in the mood of optimism. There was a label for the likes of me—a *Wahlberlinerin*—a person who chooses to become a Berliner. It doesn't mean you have to stay forever. For the present, you choose Berlin as home. Or did Berlin choose me?

In that hospital maternity ward, we nuzzled our babies, counting again and again ten tiny fingers and ten tiny toes, reassuring ourselves that all would be well for our children and that the future was bright.

The Williams family at home in Halensee

A week after Scott's entrance onto the world's stage, Charles premiered in a production of Sweet Charity on the stage of the Theater des Westens, West Berlin's operetta and musical comedy theater. He played the role of Daddy Brubeck. The local B.Z. newspaper thought it cute that this Daddy should have become a daddy once more and published a double-page spread featuring Scott and Charles.

Even as our circle of friends was expanding, Tante Susi and Onkel Werner became ever more like our own family. Children in Germany did not get immunizing shots to protect them from mumps, measles, and rubella. Children were allowed to contract these diseases, and so I seemed to be constantly on the phone with Tante Susi asking advice about how best to care for my ailing little ones. I never administered medicine or antibiotics. I was advised only to give comfort. Tante Susi had, by this time, dubbed us her "*Vize Familie.*" (vice family or second family).

Tante Susi offered advice on other matters as well. "Don't get too many things too soon in life, Ruth," she cautioned. "See, I am almost fifty now, and I have such great happiness because of my new stove." Luckily, she had yet to acquire a dishwasher because she and I held our best conversations over her kitchen sink, as she washed and I dried. There we could discuss and analyze, while holding glasses to the light and polishing them spotless.

For Germans it was important to make time to sit and chat and have meals with their friends. Work was something that interrupted their search for pleasure with those close to them. That was an important lesson we learned from them. For our part, we had fun teaching our close German friends "facies," jokes involving the face. You pulled up the outer corners of your eyes and said, "Mommy, mommy are my braids too tight?" You pressed your nose with your open palm and said, "Don't you think you're standing a little too close?" Our friends, Sepl and Inge Ruhnau and their daughter Petra roared with laughter at these jokes. Our afternoon coffee times together were full of laughter and fun and the free flow of champagne.

Germans love good conversation. Their language uses the same word for entertainment and conversation: Unterhaltungen. A good conversation is entertaining. You take an idea and discuss it and pull it apart and look at it from many sides and argue. And pour wine and drink. And argue some more. Oh, it is fun. Stimulating. That's entertainment

By the 1970s, our German was fluent enough to enjoy a good conversation. Our times with our German friends, filled with conversation, helped me through the coldest days of winter and fall and some dreary summers that were not warm at all. Being with friends made it possible for me to combat snippy salespeople and arrogant strangers with their icy stares, though I had never talked about such treatment to Berliners in my first years in the city. The acceptance and support of friends had helped me through many unpleasant encounters, including the time when the whiplike tone of the baker's wife—"*BITTE?!*"—so shocked and repelled me that I'd run back home in tears without buying the bread for the day.

Now after ten years in the country, Charles and I finally had the courage to complain directly to a Berliner about German discourtesy and rudeness, a topic often discussed among fellow foreigners.

"Just be glad you are foreigners," Sepl told us over an evening meal. "Germans are more polite to you because you are foreigners. We behave much worse toward each other."

Worse?

Well, foreigners—non-Berliners—could travel more easily in and out of the city. There were some restrictions, of course. In June 1971, we took our first family vacation to West Germany. Ten-month-old Scott had his own U.S. passport and six-year-old Lynne also carried her own U.S. passport. The children were Americans by virtue of their father's citizenship, but since Charles traveled so often apart from his children, the three U.S. citizens could not share a passport. The Americans in our little family (everyone except me) could travel through East Germany. I still held a Philippine passport, which was not valid for travel to and through East Germany.

Therefore, to reach our holiday destination in Bavaria, Scott and I flew to Hannover from Berlin, the shortest distance from Berlin to West Germany. Charles drove with Lynne in our VW Beetle to Hannover to meet us. And, finally, from there we traveled together to Bavaria. It was a roundabout way to get there, but because of my nationality a whole country called East Germany had to be circumnavigated.

Despite such hassles, we were quite content to stay in our island city of West Berlin, flying over East Germany or traveling swiftly through it occasionally to visit friends in West Germany. And on our visits back to the States, we always flew by Pan American Airlines first along the air corridor linking West Berlin to Frankfurt, and then from Frankfurt to New York City.

Our lives in the West were busy and fulfilled, and we seldom even saw the Wall. We no longer purposely went to the Wall except when visitors came. It wasn't that we were trying to ignore it, it was just that we didn't want its unpleasantness to touch us, to spoil our comfortable life.

In 1972, my father, now in retirement in Manila, decided to see the Olympic Games in Munich. On his way, he would come to visit us. After his assignment in Seoul, he had been sent as chargé at the Philippine Embassy in London, where he later presented his credentials as ambassador to the Court of St. James's. London was his last post before retirement

The passing years had done little at first to warm the icy winds that whistled through the gap between our generations, but the arrival of Lynne and Scott helped smooth the way to reconciliation—at least with my father. My parents' visits to Berlin were infrequent: once, when Lynne was seven months old; once when Scott was eleven months old.

When Dad came to our home, our children called him Lolo, grandfather in Tagalog, and he played with them all the children's games he had once played with me.

"Forehead bender, eye seer, nose smeller, mouth eater—Gallyhopper!" touching appropriate parts of the face with a forefinger, then tickling the neck to the delighted shrieks of the children.

We took Lolo to visit the outer limits of our city. We climbed the platform that let us look over the Wall at Potsdamer Platz, through the massive columns of the Brandenburg Gate, and into East Berlin. We took a boat ride from Wannsee south to where the edge of our city was marked by a line of buoys in the water. We looked across at the Wall on the opposite bank, which prevented us from seeing the people on the other side.

I pointed out the divisions of the land and lake around us. "We're in the West, Dad. And over there—that's the East." Seagulls followed our boat, calling to each other and keeping pace. They swooped to catch the pieces of bread we threw at them. They flew east, they flew west. They could land freely on either shore.

"They have no travel limits," said Dad. "Their species is smarter than ours."

Yes, the birds were smarter because they erected neither physical barriers, such as the Wall, nor emotional ones, like those that separated my father and me. Dad and I each had a role to play: he, the supportive husband to my mother; I, the determined wife to Charles. Those roles would keep us apart, and we both knew it. Dad always had a wall around him that sheltered his dignity and reserve.

I cried when we saw Dad off to London at Tempelhof Airport. Our visit had been full of fun and laughter. He was crying, too. We knew that healing had begun, but so much more time was needed. Maybe we would be given a chance for the healing to continue. Maybe not.

Usually, I never cry at farewells. There had been too many of them in my life. A farewell was not only the end of something, it was the start of something new. That was the gift of my wandering, rootless life.

Like my father and I, East and West Berlin grew a little closer in 1972. That was the year the Berlin Agreement came into effect. Now East Germans over 60 years old could visit relatives in the West for up to thirty days a year, and Philippine citizens, such as I, could travel to and through East German territory.

When Charles signed a five-month contract in spring 1972 to perform in *Kiss Me Kate* at the Theater an der Wien, we wanted to avoid a long separation and decided to move to Vienna for the length of the contract. This time, we could travel together all the way from West Berlin *through East Germany* into Austria, our VW Beetle packed snugly with five months' worth of clothes and toys.

We returned to Berlin in late summer. It was the kind of cool European summer that leaves you doubly sad, as drizzly days stretch on into autumn.

November is Berlin's gloomiest month, however, the month when the ever-present rain turns cold, the days become short, and the flower shops set out their wreaths. In November, Germans commemorate what Charles and I have somewhat irreverently named "The Dead Days." On the first Sunday in November, Germans remember all the soldiers who have died. In mid-November, workers get a holiday called Buss-und Bettag on which to repent and pray, and on the third Sunday of the eleventh month, all thoughts are meant to turn to all those who have died. November is altogether a dreadfully somber time.

To Americans, on the other hand, November means Thanksgiving. American expatriates celebrate this holiday with an exuberance not quite captured by Americans who have never left home. Emulating the Velveteen Rabbit's dream that someday I would become a real American, I savored every facet of the Thanksgiving celebration.

In 1972, we were invited to a Thanksgiving dinner in Dahlem. Ah, I thought, an authentic Thanksgiving with a big American turkey and "all the trimmings." I especially looked forward to the cranberry sauce. There is something so very American about cranberry sauce. I mean the kind that comes out of the can and lies in a dish on its side wobbling and glistening, with grooves from the sides of a can.

Alas, although the dinner was elegant and beautifully served, the cranberry sauce was not there. Only later, long after the pumpkin pies had been consumed, did our hostess realize her omission. We guests, of course, were all too polite to say we had missed it.

The next Sunday we were telling Tante Susi and Onkel Werner about our Thanksgiving dinner, and Onkel said, "Thanksgiving. *Ja-ja,* I learned about Thanksgiving in America."

"Onkel, you've been to America?"

"*Ja-ja,* I was a prisoner of war in Louisiana. We prisoners were treated very well, and we were served a Thanksgiving dinner. *Ja-ja.* Cranberry sauce. They served cranberry sauce with the dinner."

I looked at Onkel with new eyes. A prisoner of war? *My* Onkel? I did not question him further then but promised myself that I would someday ask him more. But that someday never came for he would die before I could bring myself to ask about his imprisonment. Whatever the larger truth might be, his kindness to us is part of the truth, too. And to us, the important part of that whole truth is that we had grown to love him, for he had loved us first.

There were always reminders of the war, some more horrifying than others. In early 1973, Charles put on a tuxedo to give his first full-length solo Lieder concert at the St. Michaelsheim, the church headquarters of the Johannische Church with whose choir he frequently performed as soloist. Tante Susi and Onkel Werner were there, of course, sitting all smiles in the middle of the front row. I spoke with Tante Susi at the intermission. "It is going very well," she said. "Charles's German is just fine. I can understand every word." I was very pleased.

After the concert, Onkel had gone to fetch their coats, and Tante was standing in the corridor, looking about as if she were lost.

"Tante?" (I hated to disturb her reverie.)

"I know this place. I've been here before, I think."

Suddenly, a crowd of smiling faces surrounded me, my hand was being wrung, my shoulders squeezed, and I heard myself saying, " . . . glad you enjoyed it . . . nice of you to come . . . yes, he is entertaining, isn't he? . . . must get together . . . say hi to your mother."

Not far away, I saw Charles surrounded by well-wishers. His arms were full of bouquets and more flowers were being pressed upon him. Professor Garay stood beside him, clearly pleased with the performance and bursting with pride.

Because Lynne took music classes offered by the Johannische Church and Scott had joined the children's pottery class, I found myself at the St. Michaelsheim almost every Saturday. While there, I sometimes wondered about the expression on Tante Susi's face on the night of Charles's concert. Something about the place had awakened in her a lingering memory. It made me wonder about the building housing the concert hall. I began to investigate.

My research revealed that the St. Michaelsheim had once been the Mendelssohn family estate. It was built around the turn of the century, and it was known as a cultural center where the famous, the wealthy, and the intellectual could gather for evenings of good music and conversation. In 1938, the building was confiscated by the Wehrmacht, the German military, and the Mendelssohn brothers, Franz and Robert, were forced to flee.

In 1945, the building was first occupied by Russian troops, then American soldiers, and finally the British forces, who turned it into a school. In 1957, the Johannischer Aufbauwerk e.V. took it over and made it their church headquarters.

I began to read books about Berlin. I was fascinated by Christopher Isherwood's *Berlin Stories*, for Isherwood had lived at Nollendorf Platz, half a block away from our former apartment. And I read *The Last Battle* by Cornelius Ryan.

I learned that the House Dahlem where all those nuns had been raped by invading Russian soldiers was around the corner from where we had enjoyed those fabulous dinners with American friends. And Winterfeld Strasse, the last point from which telegraphed messages were issued just before the city fell, was where I used to do my shopping at the open market on Tuesdays and Fridays.

I became aware of the history of the city, and everywhere, on street corners and buildings, I suddenly sensed the presence of forces and feelings from a past still not at rest. I thought of all the women I knew now in their late forties who would have been young girls that fateful spring of 1945, when Russian troops first entered the city to rape and plunder and rape again: our pediatrician, who was now taking English lessons from me; oh God . . . Mama in Augsburg, and *oh my God* . . . Tante Susi. What had they done? Where could they have hidden? Did they get away? Oh, surely they did. Please, please say they did. It was almost too hideous to think about.

How glibly I asked the question of my student. "Were you in Berlin in the spring of 1945?" She told me that during the first frightful weeks of the Russian occupation, her mother had hidden her in a huge bin in the cellar, buried over her head in coal. Every evening, she came out of her hiding place to eat a meal, wash up, and exercise a bit. I did not remember to correct her vocabulary or grammar—I could only listen in horror.

I was on my way to Tante Susi's one Friday. We had telephoned earlier in the week, each of us bemoaning the fact that life was too busy. We seemed to have so little time for conversation. We would set aside Friday morning for some coffee and companionship.

I was driving along Martin-Luther-Strasse, heading toward Steglitz. I was anticipating that easy swing right, then the circling left around Innsbrucker Platz's grassy circle. But the road kept going straight. Suddenly, I found myself in the middle of the Steglitzer shopping district.

What happened to Innsbrucker Platz? What happened to the circle? Where was the grass? I could not question too deeply, for the road was unfamiliar and needed my attention.

"There's still a sign there that says Innsbrucker Platz," said Tante Susi, as we were sitting down to coffee.

"But it is all so ugly now," I said. "And it looks like they are building some sort of overpass. There is a lot of dust and construction going on. What about that beautiful space and the sparrows you could feed? And what about the crocuses? Oh, Tante, what about the crocuses? How will we ever believe that spring will come again?"

Tante Susi seemed amused by my complaints. She had no way of knowing that I had promised my future, older self that I would come back to Innsbrucker Platz just to see the crocuses. "There will always be ways to believe that spring will come," she said calmly.

"Oh Tante, let me tell you what I found out," I said. And with thoughtless enthusiasm, I presented her with the fruits of my research about the St. Michaelsheim and how the Mendelssohn brothers fled, and the British came and the Russians.

"Were you in the city when the Russians came?"

"Yes." And without hesitation or even emotion, she proceeded to tell me her story.

Susi and her two sisters had gathered with their mother and father in the cellar of their apartment. "When the Russians came in, our father tried to shield us with his own body. We were told they had just shot the father next door for trying to shield his daughter. We did not want our father shot dead, so we allowed ourselves to be taken. In front of our mother and father, each of us was raped three times."

"But . . . but," I faltered. I didn't know what to say. Tante went on, "Right afterward we went to the hospital to make sure everything was all right." And the memories continued to flow. "I, like so many young people, had belonged to the Arbeitsdienst, [the mandatory civilian workforce established by the Nazi regime] you know." I shook my head. I knew nothing.

"That means that after the war, people like me were regarded as having been good Nazis." My mouth hung open. "We were given the worst and hardest jobs. The Russians who first occupied the St. Michaelsheim building had used the bathtubs there as toilets. I had the job of cleaning out the tubs." She actually smiled. "There was a young American soldier posted outside the bathroom door to guard me. He felt so sorry for me that he lit one cigarette after another and handed them to me while I worked. You know how valuable cigarettes were in those days."

All I could do was gasp. Tante saw my distress and comforted me with, "When I think about it now, it seems as though it happened to someone else at another time and another place. We cannot continue with life if we forever dwell on the unpleasant things that happen to us."

I could not speak. I put my arms around her and said nothing. I thought about Charles's concert at the St. Michaelsheim and how Tante Susi's being there to hear him sing had stirred old memories. I thought about Professor Garay, his jacket's long sleeves hiding tattooed numbers that enumerated human cruelty and wrongdoing almost too dreadful to recount. And I thought about the music of this country, the Lieder, those German art songs that Charles sang with such joy, charming a Berlin audience. I thought about this rich and abiding city within whose Wall the destinies of Tante Susi, Onkel Werner, and Professor Ernst Garay were intertwined.

I wondered about my destiny. Did it lie here, too? As much as I continued to hold a little glow of hope that America would one day be my real home, I could not now erase eleven years of life and family love that seemed to be holding me here. In the fluid community of American transients, multi-national and multi-ethnic people, we'd often ask ourselves, where is home? Where you hang your hat. Where you speak the language. Where you are when your children are small. For now, Berlin was home.

I was constantly learning new facts and gaining new insights into the city—sometimes in very unexpected ways. A sign, in stilted official wording, was taped to the wall beside the mailboxes in the entranceway of our apartment building on Seesener Strasse one summer day in 1976. The Municipal Sanitation Department would pick up old furniture, old clothing, household items, trash, or other discarded things too large for the garbage cans. West Berlin was giving citizens a chance to rid their attics and cupboards of unwanted junk. We would do more than just discard bulky trash; we would free cluttered living space for use again.

We were instructed to put our discards on the sidewalk the day before pickup day. We sighed with relief, for the woman who owned the apartment before us—that jovial woman with whom we had knocked back the thimblelike glasses of Bismarck Schnapps—had left our walk-in pantry stuffed with junk. The walk-in pantry was a peculiarly narrow room called the maid's room, and it adjoined the kitchen. It had a mere slit of a window, barely eight inches wide, that looked out across the back court-yard. I wondered how such a space, little more than a closet, could possibly be anybody's room. But Berliner friends assured us it really was the maid's room. The large, deep overhead shelf was used as a loft bed for a nanny or maid. Below it was just space enough for one wardrobe.

I imagined a cozy nest, a safe hiding place, away from the battles of the world. And then I learned that many Jews on the run had been hidden in rooms such as this.

On the day before our appointed pickup day, we hauled out the junk. When we moved it, we sneezed away the accumulated dust of years.

Piles of tattered cardboard, stacks of old newspapers, old stained and torn curtains, curtain rods, a very large cooking pot for laun-dry (Germans like to boil cotton laundry on top of the stove, like eggs, because they believe it gets laundry really, really clean), two broken chairs, lots of old clothes, four teacups chipped beyond repair, and two five-gallon cans of butter. Printed on the lids of the cans were the words: "From the people of the United States of America to the people of Germany." The butter must once have been part of a CARE package.

One container had been opened, and about two pounds of its contents removed. The butter was rancid through and through, so we threw out the can. The other can was still unopened. Curious, we opened it. It didn't smell sour, but its color was a light orange, so we threw it out, too. In Berlin we seemed always to be uncover-ing the remnants of war.

I thought back to a day in my elementary school in San Fran-cisco, when everyone said that the war was over. My second-grade class packed a CARE package for a place called Germany. Our teacher let each of us hold one item, a box of animal crackers or a bar of soap. And, in turn, we placed our items in the package. Our teacher said that these things were going to the victims of oppression.

In Berlin, now, in the mid-1970s, I looked at cans of butter that someone somewhere had packed into a CARE package. I imagined a war-weary family opening the box of gifts from people across the sea—winners in war sending gifts to the vanquished. Then I thought of Charles, carefully packing carnival prizes. At least at a carnival it is clear who has won and who has lost.

Throwing out unwanted junk, we were seeing evidence of how a family once fought off hunger. In the days of scarcities after the war, our apartment predecessor had determined never again to want for butter; yet thirty years later that once precious butter joined the rising mountains of trash on the pavement outside.

From our Berlin balcony we had a fine view of what we called The Junk Day Show. From the doors of the apartment houses along our street, people brought out old trunks, pieces of cupboards, and bits of beds, broken television sets, radios, and lamps, forgotten vases, once-proud wall plaques, posters, paintings, and trophies, the very stuff of yard sales in America.

"So!" they said as they deposited their junk on the pavement. They wiped their dirty hands on their jeans and returned to their cellars or storerooms for more.

Later in the afternoon, the scavengers arrived. A man carrying a sack inspected the bundles of old clothing. "Aha!" he said, as he picked out a tie and moved on. A dark-haired woman sifted through boxes of rhinestone jewelry, pocketed a piece, and moved on. A very fat woman, pushing a dilapidated wicker baby buggy full of yellow cloth came by. She was looking for more yellow material, but we had none in front of our house, so she moved on. A truck rattled down the street, bearing tin tubs. Yes, there was a tin container in front of the next building. Giving a whistle of triumph, the driver tossed the tin onto his truck and drove off with a clatter.

We had been given old wooden chairs with leather seats, which we no longer wanted. We took them out on Junk Day. The chairs' legs never touched the pavement. As soon as the chairs saw the sunlight, three people came along and carried them away.

Over the years, Junk Day became a game. Young couples would wait for Junk Day to see what they could add to their homes. We knew an American couple who completely furnished their apartment with the gleanings of Junk Day. Neighbors took turns helping each other carry out bulky items, and at times one person's trash would become another person's newfound treasure.

I was descending the stairs with an armload of old newspapers when our neighbor across the landing said, "Ruth, are you not looking for a sideboard? I think there is one under the tree three doors down." I went to inspect it. Sure enough, it was just what we were looking for. I don't know how long it had been in someone's attic, but—after its top and knobs were replaced and it had been given a good polish—it would soon be gracing our dining room.

Before the piles of discarded things were hauled away, the vandals arrived. In their hurry to find hidden treasure, some people would rummage through the piles of trash, tossing things over their heads. If they didn't like a glass or a vase, they'd smash it.

Someone inspected our old television set. He removed its back covering, took out the tubes, and went away. Later, another person kicked in the screen.

When Sanitation Department trucks came to pick up the junk, workers had to clean the mess left behind by scavengers and vandals. I believe Junk Day was eventually abandoned because the sight of people picking through rubbish brought back too many unhappy memories of the days before prosperity.

The mid-1970s, which I call The Junk Day years, saw a supportive community evolve in our apartment house. Although Charles was away on engagements in West Germany much of the time, I never wanted for friendship or companionship. And if I needed a plumber or an electrician, our neighbors were there with offers of help.

I wanted to contribute to the community, too, so I expanded my teaching to tutor to the school-age children, especially those preparing for matriculation to university, for which English was a requirement. Although freed in English from the need to choose from among 16 definite articles, my charges were often stumped by the simple, progressive, interrogative, or negative forms of English verbs. My pupils and I would hunch over the dining-room table to find the right verb form and together enjoy the novelty of saying something in a new way.

One 14-year-old often brought me large bouquets of flowers. He worked hard but always had, at-the-ready, a tiny vial of liquid called Tintenkiller (an ink eradicator). A little glass applicator that reminded me of an old-fashioned bottle of Mercurochrome allowed him to bleach out mistakes written with a fountain pen. He was keen to get things right, right away. I wanted him to fail a little, to see his mistake, and understand it, not bleach it away and write over it. But he came to every lesson armed with Tintenkiller.

I also gave individual adult English conversation lessons at home. My own spoken German was improving slowly, and often, I learned just as much from a student as my student learned from me.

Our pediatrician came to me once a week for English lessons. Our conversations often evoked memories of the years immediately after World War II.

"When the bombing was all over, we returned to our apartment. It was *almost* completely destroyed. But in a *Hängeboden*, er . . . what is *Hängeboden?*"

"An attic where laundry is hung to dry," I suggested.

"Yes, in such a place, there was one thing left *unzerstört.*"

"There was one thing left intact," I said.

"Yes. Intact. And it was the dollhouse that my father had build for me when I was nine years old. I remember that Advent season very well. We had not much money. Every evening instead of taking me on his lap and reading to me, my father locked himself inside the dining-room. And I could hear sawing and hammer."

"Hammer-ing," I said.

"Then on Christmas Eve I went into the living room, and it was there. Oh, it was beautiful: a whole house and two little dolls; little dishes even and a fireplace and all the furniture and little lamps."

"But after the bombing you found it still intact." My words brought her back to the present.

"After the war, mother and I were alone. My mother took the dollhouse to the black market and sold it to an American army officer for four cartons of American cigarettes. You know that then one carton of twenty packs of cigarettes was worth 1,000 marks. So then we had 4,000 marks and that paid the tuition for my medical studies."

Another student was simply keen on, as she put it, extending her vocabulary. She read every book in English that she could get hands on. She came from a well-known Berlin family and already spoke excellent English. I enjoyed making a pleasant occasion out of our hour together, and sometimes I served tea.

She came to one lesson with an English paperback book. She was a bit irritated, and pouting, said, "There is a word in this book that is not in my dictionary."

I poured tea into two cups and passed her a plate of dainty cakes. Then I took the book and studied its cover. A woman in a black-lace negligee was reclining upon a sofa. A deeply plunging neckline revealed cleavage and generous bosoms. In one hand she held a revolver, which was pointed steadily at a man entering the room. I had never heard of the author.

"Here is the word," said my student, finding the page. "C-u-n-t. Please what means *cunt*?"

I kept my face serene. "*Cunt* is a vulgar word, which means the female sex organ."

"Aha," said my student easily. "In German, it is *Votze*."

I raised my eyebrows. "*Votze!*" Perhaps I said it a little too loudly. "Why, I see that word so often on the walls of buildings and in elevators, but I thought it meant 'fart.'"

"Oh, no," said my student, now assuming the role of teacher. "That would be *Furz,* spelled with an *r.*"

"Well, we've both learned something today," I said smoothly. "How is your tea?"

"Oh, it is very fine, thank you," she said. And I passed her a dainty petit four.

The occupants of our apartment building (eight apartments in the front wing and eight apartments in the rear) joined forces for two annual events: the Sommerfest and the Christmas Eve courtyard concert.

On a chosen day in summer, we organized a Sommerfest. In the courtyard, we set out tables and chairs, prepared coffee, cake, and other eats, and gathered for an afternoon of companionship. Sometimes the older children staged puppet shows for the tiny ones. Sometimes families included visiting relatives, and I met aunts and uncles in their sixties who had come from that other part of town, that other Germany—the mysterious eastern half of this city and country in which I had now spent more years than any other country in my erratic and fractured embassy-hopping life. Unconsciously, I was becoming a part of this place. I knew what was expected, but I also enjoyed being a little bit on the outside of things. I still was—and always would be—a foreigner.

I'd observe these strangers from the East, sitting quietly surrounded by chatter and laughter. Unlike those bandana-wearing Bavarian marketplace women of my first year in Germany, who stared at me with unabashed curiosity, these visitors from the East were unsure of themselves and shy. Always, they were the quiet ones. I called them the Tawny Tantes because their clothing was notable for its drabness. Sometimes I'd catch one casting shy glances at me.

One Sommerfest day, after the tables had been set and pots of hot coffee brought out, the heavens suddenly opened. The deluge drove us scurrying and dripping back indoors. Minutes later, undaunted, we reorganized. We set up tables and chairs, plates, cups,

saucers, and silverware on every landing of our four-story building. The stairwell was never so merry, the wisecracks and laughter
never so hearty. We had defied the elements. Our plans and our
enjoyment would continue without pause. And in the shuffle, I
found myself seated next to an auntie from the East.

Sommerfest in the courtyard

"Yes, I am allowed to come over, now that I am sixty years
old," she explained.

"Do you like it here?" I asked.

"Oh, yes. It is very beautiful."

We didn't know what else to say to each other. We just smiled
and drank our coffee.

The West Berlin counterparts of these East Berlin seniors, the
sixty-or seventy-year-old women who occupied the small apartments in the back wing of our building, I referred to not as Tantes
but as Omas (grandmas). They lived alone and had no relatives
among the other apartment dwellers. I would see these white-
haired Omas sitting alone, framed by their living-room windows,
looking out on to the courtyard or across at me. Seldom did they

join us for the summer celebrations, preferring to remain at home, observing the life and laughter below from their windowsill vantage points.

In winter, these senior residents of the back court had veritable box seats for the other annual apartment house community event, the Christmas Eve courtyard concert. On the evening of December 5, the day before Nikolaus Day, little children put out their polished shoes for the coming of St. Nikolaus. Children were told that if they found a little gift or a piece of candy in their shoes on the morning of Nikolas Day, it was a sign that they had been good. A piece of coal in a shoe meant that a child had not been good. On December 6, a poster announcing the midday Christmas Eve concert was taped on the wall of the spacious entranceway.

On December 24, the flurry of pre-Christmas preparations—the shopping, the wrapping, the hiding of presents, and writing of little tags—was accompanied now by sounds of musical instruments and songs wafting through the courtyard air. Often the final rehearsing of songs took place in our living room. Then near midday, a hush descended. And promptly at noon, a trumpet solo opened the program.

Every window looking out on to the courtyard was filled with one or more spectators. People had stopped to enjoy the Christmas Eve concert, a half-hour program of instrumental music and singing (solos, quartets, or chorus). Sometimes Lynne would play the flute, and Scott would play the gong. Some years a children's dance group was formed, and when they were the appropriate ages, Lynne and Scott became part of the dancing group, too.

Whenever he was home at Christmas time, Charles, bundled against the cold in hat, scarf, a warm coat, and boots, always joined our neighbors in the snow to sing the story of Christmas: "Go tell it on-ze mountains, ova-ze hills and eff-ry whe-e . . ."

Charles and I were beginning to enjoy compliments about how well we spoke German. The children spoke German as well as any child born in Germany. My own experience with a mother tonuge made me worry about our children's English-language fluency, for I had grown up in a household where the mother tongue of my parents (Tagalog) was not taught to me. Therefore, I reached adulthood unable to speak my native language. That inability severed me irreparably from my roots, and it made me determined to teach my children to speak American English as well as any child born in America. The strictest rule in our home was the speaking of English at all times, except of course when a neighbor child came to play.

Christmas Eve concert in the courtyard

There were places in West Berlin where I could expose the children to American English. As civilians, we could attend church services at the American Community Chapel on Hüttenweg in the American Sector of town. And we had many American friends who lived in U.S. Army housing. In Zehlendorf, adjacent to Clayallee, the wide boulevard named after the American general Lucius D. Clay, stood a transplanted piece of suburban America. Row upon row of duplexes lined up behind fenceless front lawns, tidy sidewalks, and well-paved streets. In summer, children on bicycles and roller skates played in the streets for cars drove by infrequently.

America, and all it symbolized to the beleaguered city, could be sampled here.

I liked to visit friends there as often as possible to allow the children to speak English away from home and play with American children. I pretended I was really in America where I remembered life was not so structured, where salespeople were helpful, where I could be myself—whatever *that* was.

How convenient it was to send Lynne out to play without worrying about the traffic and the heavy front door that led from the sidewalk to the building's entranceway; and four-year-old Scott loved running freely in the backyard.

But not every aspect of American culture was positive. On our way home from one all-day visit, Scott had fallen asleep as soon as we turned left into Clayallee and headed toward Halensee. Nine-year-old Lynne, bubbly as usual, said, "Mommy, you know what?"

"What?"

"I'm a Nigger."

I gripped the steering wheel more tightly. Now don't react, Ruth, I said to myself. "Oh?"I inquired smoothly.

Lynne went on chattering in that happy little way of hers, but I wasn't listening. Charles had an acting role in a play in Stuttgart and also had performances in the musical *The Me Nobody Knows* in Bremen, but the next time Charles came home, he'd have to speak with her seriously, man-to-girl, about who she was and what *Nigger* meant and what *Negro* meant and what *black* meant and *America* and *grandmother* and *grandfather* and *pride* and *slavery* and . . . Oh, Goodness! But that was *his* job, I said to myself. Not mine. Some-day I'd teach the children about Spanish and American colonialism in the Philippines.

Some months later, Lynne celebrated her tenth birthday. Her favorite toy was the Barbie doll, so we gave her a Barbie and kind friends had contributed all the various accouterments somehow due to the Little Lady of Matell. One American girlfriend had given Lynne a Francine doll. On opening her present, Lynne exclaimed, "Oh, goody! A Nigger Barbie!!" And yes, when that happened, Charles was out of town again, but he was coming home the next day.

I cornered him in the kitchen while the children were watching television in the living room and told him of the two incidents. "This Black awareness stuff is your department. I wouldn't know where to begin," I said.

Lynne called out, "Look Daddy! A Nigger singer!" I jerked my thumb toward the living room. We couldn't have prayed for a clearer window of opportunity.

"That is a *black* singer," corrected Charles entering the living room with slow and dignified steps. Then, in his best stage voice, he declared, "Lynne—Black is beautiful!"

Lynne eyed him with puzzlement. "Black is beautiful? No it isn't. It's yucky!"

Charles and I left the room, laughing and crying, composed ourselves, and returned. Our children looked at us, then at each other, shrugged their young shoulders, and continued watching television. Without saying a word to each other about it, Charles and I decided to allow the children to discover racism in their own lives, in their own way. Their world would be so different from the one we knew. There was no clear way to prepare them for what lay ahead.

The life of a young, growing family, in any country, is a busy, complex matter. But in Europe life stops—for the World Cup. In summer 1974, our son and daughter joined neighbor children before television screens, shrieking and yelling, as West Germany's soccer team advanced to the finals of the World Cup. That summer, the final match was played in Munich, but an earlier first-round game had been played in Hamburg and pitted West Germany against East Germany. Because of this special event, 1,500 carefully chosen East German soccer fans had been allowed to cross over into West Germany to attend the match. Hamburg's Volkspark stadium had thundered prophetically that day, as rooters for both sides chanted in unison, "Deutschland! Deutschland! Deutschland!"

What an intriguing thought, a Germany united. Why, it would change everything, wouldn't it? The thought came. The thought went. The thought tried valiantly to return, but it wasn't allowed to live long in my mind, crowded as it was already with everyday responsibilities. A united Germany . . . well, of all things . . .

I had become well aware of anti-German feelings among foreigners living in Germany. I often joined in gripe sessions about Germans, typical Germans, we called them, and their aggressive, rude manners. Yet in the intimate setting of their homes or in our own home where we met as good friends, we loved their company.

So I was smiling with my lips, but my brows were knitted in a frown when I saw my two children jumping about joyfully in the summer sunshine with other Berliner children, chanting, "*Wir sind Weltmeister! Wir sind Weltmeister!*" For although West Germany had lost that early game in Hamburg, known as the Brothers' Battle, the Federal Republic of Germany (West Germany) would later face Holland for the championship and be victorious. The word *Weltmeister* means champion, but a transliteration of the word is Master of the World.

Scott was smitten by the game of soccer. We watched him growing and playing soccer on the sidewalk below our balcony almost every day. His coaches were the older boys who lived one floor above us. For hours, they practiced and dribbled and passed and shot goals. Had we been living in the United States, Scott would probably be playing baseball. Soccer had not yet become a popular sport in the States.

Wait! What about America? What about finding a real home? Not this visitor, observer-on-the-sidelines condition. Don't you want to be home, Ruth? Yes. But first there was the shopping, the next meal, the homework to check, the next *story* uniquely Berlin to be dazzled by.

In the United States, it is polite for guests not to overstay their visit. Let the host and hostess get some rest. In Germany, it is a compliment to the host if you stay long and loud and consume everything in sight. Our one-year adventure had stretched to a dozen. How long could this impermanence last? My place for now was with Charles and our children. However long we'd remain, it wouldn't be permanent—unlike the Wall.

One day in 1976, I was standing on our balcony, overlooking the sidewalk on Seesener Strasse, watching Scott playing soccer and at the same time monitoring eleven-year-old Lynne's piano practice in the room from which the balcony opened and thinking how quickly the children were growing up. Was this blossoming young girl the baby that we had carried so easily from party to party that humid summer of rich and spicy food back in 1966?

Our children were two Berlin-born Americans who only knew one half of the city. They spoke fluent German, well marked by the Berliner dialect, as well as English, though some of their phrasing was unidiomatic. They knew their heritage stretched across to North America and Asia, with one set of grandparents living in Dayton, Ohio, and another in Manila. But they had yet to see the eastern half of the city of their birth. It was time to take Lynne and Scott to the other side of the Wall.

CHAPTER 4

drüben (over there)

Our only contact with East Berlin had occurred during Charles's student days, when he had occasionally crossed over to the East to buy music scores. Unlike most residents of West Berlin, we had no aunts or uncles, no grandmothers or cousins who lived on the other side. Once many years before, however, Charles had met an East Berliner named Detlev, the cousin of a good friend in West Berlin and had promised to return someday. We got word to Detlev that we planned to visit East Berlin.

Weeks beforehand we asked friends in the West, "What do you bring when you visit people *drüben* [over there]?" They answered: coffee, chocolate, soap, and chewing gum. East Germans, we were told, had a hard time finding these items, and they were always appreciated. Coffee in the East costed more than four times what it did in the West.

It was only fifteen minutes by car from our apartment to Checkpoint Charlie, the crossing point between West and East Berlin to be used by foreigners. To process through on foot, we had to be checked four times by the border guards. We declared the money we had with us, declared the goods we brought with us, declared the day a lovely day.

"Why are they looking in my bag?" asked Scott. We wanted to say, "They have to make sure you haven't hidden any anti-East German propaganda in the chewing gum." But we answered, "They want to see how much gum we brought."

"But it's none of their business."

"Sh-sh-sh. They are just curious."

Detlev and his family were waiting twenty feet from the final passport control point. It had taken thirty minutes to cross the street, to process through the controls, to traverse the one city block thickness of Wall, to go from one world to another.

"Is this another country?" asked Lynne.

"Sort of. But they speak German here, too." It was not the time or place to delve into the problems of the German Question.

Detlev and Ursula had two sons: Peter, age six, and Jens, twelve. The two six-year-olds became friends immediately. These little ones didn't know or care about differences in economic systems, about different ideologies, or different political theories. At first, Jens fixed Lynne with a soulful gaze, but she ignored him. They, too, did not care about politics. They were simply being two pre-adolescents.

Charles had sung in a concert the night before and, as is the custom, received several huge bouquets of flowers. We brought one bouquet to Ursula.

"Oh, my God!" said Detlev, in dismay. "I wanted so much to give you a bouquet of flowers, Ruth, but there doesn't seem to be any flowers in the city. They've all been sold to the West for profit. None are left for the citizens here."

I tried hard to conceal the discomfort of my questioning thoughts. Profit? Here in the East? Wasn't this Communist? Didn't that mean state-run . . . . er, everything? It was too early in our visit to ask such questions.

Detlev excused himself and left us as we continued walking to the Konrads' apartment.

The family lived on the twelfth floor of a twenty-floor block of apartments. Their apartment was small. The boys shared a room. Detlev's layouts and designs (he was a commercial artist) were stashed under the bed in the master bedroom. There was a living room–dining room with adjoining kitchenette.

Ursula's azaleas seemed to be doing well, despite the fact that the apartment didn't get much sun. I thought of my flowering plants back in the West. They never did well, while my philodendron and ivy enjoyed luxuriant growth. "We get lots of sun in our apartment," I said. "Ursula, you must come . . ." I never finished the sentence. I wanted to say, "You must come over and look at my house plants and tell me what I'm doing wrong."

That would be the first of the many unfinished sentences I would utter that day. For, of course, Ursula could not come to my house. We could visit the Konrads, but the Konrads could not visit us, not until they reached the age of sixty. How ridiculous to start planning for that day now.

Detlev arrived, triumphantly waving a paper bag of warm breakfast buns.

"Very fresh! The baker is a good friend of mine. I told him I had visitors from the West. He let me go around to the side. I didn't have to line up. You should have seen the line!" I thought of the pictures I had seen of people lining up to buy even the most ordinary things in the East. Little did I know that one day I would be lining up for ordinary goods, too.

Typical of such family visits, we split up into interest groups. Jens gave up trying to capture Lynne's attention and joined the younger boys downstairs to play soccer. The fathers discussed the hazards of being an artist in any political system. Lynne, Ursula, and I were in the kitchenette. I gave Ursula the coffee but was surprised to see that we were drinking instant coffee that day.

Ursula said, "It's not that we don't like filtered coffee, it's just that my porcelain filter holder broke. I've searched and searched, but they are just not to be found in any store. We can buy the filter paper, but what good is the paper, if you can't buy the porcelain part?"

I thought of my porcelain filter holder at the back of my kitchen cupboard a short distance away. "What if I sent you one?"

"The package would probably be opened, and it might be confiscated. Better not risk it."

Later in the afternoon we took the elevator to the roof of the Konrads' apartment building. From there we could look across into West Berlin. The Axel Springer publishing house, one of the largest in West Germany, stood just on the other side of the Wall. We could see the Schoeneberger Rathaus, where President Kennedy had made his famous speech. In the distance, we could see the Funkturm, West Berlin's radio-tower landmark.

How close we were. I noticed that Jens was struggling to overcome his shyness. He wanted to ask us a question. "What is it, Jens?" I said

"Once, I saw helicopters with green and red smoke coming out of them and people with parachutes jumping out of planes over there." He pointed in the direction of Tempelhof.

"That must have been the Tempelhof Open House. Once a year the U.S. Air Force opens the gates of the Tempelhof Central Air Base to the Berlin public for a day of aerial displays. And you can buy American ice cream, hot dogs, and hamburgers," I explained. But Jens wasn't really listening. He just kept looking wistfully in the direction of Tempelhof.

The children did not have to miss any of their favorite television shows that evening, for no mere Wall could stop electronic signals beamed from the western side of town. So, seated on the floor of a small East Berlin apartment that evening, two American children and two East Berlin children enjoyed *Little House on the Prairie* and *The Muppet Show*. The voices of Laura, Mrs. Olson, Kermit, and Miss Piggy had all been dubbed into German.

I thought about the stories I had heard of East German children being reported to central authorities for their "crime" of watching West German television. Neither Ursula nor Detlev seemed concerned about the television being tuned to a West Berlin channel.

How often during that visit and subsequent visits would I suppress my inquiring thoughts? How subtly was I experiencing a political oppression from which I was actually free?

It was dark when we retraced our steps back across the barriers, back to our free island. Before saying good-bye, the Konrads pressed upon us two half-meter lengths of top quality Hungarian salami, an expensive delicacy in the West. In a conspiratorial whisper, they said, "Better cut it up into shorter pieces, then they won't suspect that you will sell it." I'd never sell such tasty salami. I'd keep it for my family and share it with friends. The lengths were carefully wrapped in aluminum foil that was wrinkled and stiff; you knew it had been used often before.

Processing back through the checkpoint, we declared the goods we had with us: four quarter-meter lengths of salami; a toy car that Peter had given Scott. Nothing subversive here. We were allowed through.

A hilarious kind of lightness infected our mood as we crossed back We passed the sign saying: "You are entering the American Sector." We had seen signs like this for years, but this evening it made us all dissolve into giggles. Charles performed a wiggly leap into the air. The children tried to copy him, and I just roared with laughter and relief. We were safe now, back in the American Sector. We were back home.

Singing jobs for Charles, by 1976, were many, varied, and better paying, but still irregular. Sometimes we would see work for weeks, even months in advance. The feast times when work was plentiful were happy. Debts could be paid and much-needed items finally repaired or bought. During the famine times, the inevitable spaces in between when no work was available, I'd write poems. My poems were not for sale. Rather, the momentary escape with the muse into that middle space where creativity is awakened gave balance to the mundane world of financial worry. Every day and every week we were so involved in preparing for the next concert or planning the next low-cost meal that we had little time to worry about the uncertainty of work for Charles.

Charles was a member of Der Klimperkasten, a troupe of ten to twelve cabaret performers who wrote and performed their own works in song and recitation, and interpreted the works of such authors as Brecht, Tucholsky, Kaestner, and Hollander.

One night after a performance with Der Klimperkasten, Charles slid his weary body into bed beside me saying, "Honey, there was a man in the audience tonight who is in charge of a whole theater club. He has offered me two solo concerts. He arranges concerts, publicizes them to his club's 10,000 members, and makes tickets available to them."

"What?" I was wide awake now.

"Two solo concerts . . . ," said Charles as he fell asleep, forcing me to hold my questions until morning.

Later that year, Charles sang a concert of spirituals at the Kaiser Wilhelm Memorial Church, and the following year, the concert was repeated. Both performances were sold out. He began doing a one-man show at the Charlottenburg Ratskeller, where the Klimperkasten performed regularly. During this time, Charles was also singing the role of Sportin' Life in productions of *Porgy and Bess* in Essen and Lübeck, as well as playing the part of Paul in *Kiss Me Kate* in Düsseldorf and Munich.

While flying between Berlin and West Germany, he often met another American performer, John Waddell, who was traveling around Germany pursuing a similar career.

"We really must do something together someday," said Charles when they met again by chance at an airport. The idea grew.

In summer 1976, Charles and John began rehearsals for a two-man show. In October, they opened at the Uraniahaus in West Berlin with their show called *Broadway Showtime*. It had a two-day run. On the first night, the Uraniahaus was half full. On the second night, the Uraniahaus was only a third full. The show was not a financial success. The names of Williams and Waddell had not yet caught the public's attention.

Charles and John continued to rehearse and polish their show. In November, invitations were sent out to producers, agents, press, and celebrities of Munich's high society by Bill Millie, the show's choreographer. Said one agent later, "We didn't know what it was. It could have been a troupe of little seven-year-old girls for all we knew." The invitation said simply, "William Millie presents *Broadway Showtime*."

On opening night a three-piece band struck up *The Entertainer* and John Waddell and Charles Williams came running from the wings down to the footlights. They sang *The Entertainer* in duet: Charles, the lyric baritone; John, the bass baritone. The audience applauded enthusiastically.

Two numbers later, the band went into march tempo. John and Charles marked time at stage center and broke into *Ein Freund, ein guter Freund,* an old (really old) German favorite, an evergreen, a memory-evoking German hit of yesteryear to tug at the strings of even the most petrified of Teutonic hearts.

A gasp ran through the audience, then cautious giggles. (Dared the Germans show delight at these foreigners singing *their* song?) A laugh, and then applause and more laughter. John and Charles warmed to the feedback. They swung into one old German favorite after another, *Veronica der Linz ist da, Fräulein Pardon, Das ist der Frühling von Berlin.* The spectators sat entranced, and Charles and John knew they'd captured their audience.

The two-hour show continued with numbers from musicals, blues, and spirituals, as well as big production dance numbers, all liberally sprinkled with gags, jokes, and offhand patter, both men speaking fluent German. The years of experience were paying off. They gave the audience what it wanted: music and dance; jokes and repartee. And the audience screamed its approval.

The *Tageszeitung München* wrote, " . . . they dance as brilliantly as they sing . . . two delightfully charming Pied Pipers." Said the *Münchener Merkur,* "The entertainers transported their audience to Broadway."

A month later, at a New Year's Eve gala performance, Waddell and Williams played to a sold-out house at the Theater 76 in der Leopoldstrasse. The *Abend Zeitung* called it "The Super-Show in the Theater 76—this is the show of the year!"

In April 1977, Waddell and Williams made their first television appearance on the *Rudi Carrell Show,* a popular television program of live entertainment. Later that month, they presented their *Broadway Showtime* at the Opera House in Graz, Austria. The critics in Graz raved.

Offers to appear on television, at theaters in Germany, Switzerland, Austria, and Holland came swiftly, and there was suddenly more work, and well-paying work, than the two performers had ever enjoyed before.

John Waddell (left) and Charles in rehearsal for "Broadway Showtime"

In late summer 1977, Charles and John performed in Dresden in East Germany. They had been invited by the Dresden Kulturpalast for five days of performances. Although audiences were responsive, hotel management was snippy, and the general atmosphere of the city was dreary and defeatist.

The five-day experience in Dresden left Charles and John saddened. Charles told me, "Those people over there have given up. Everything is run by the state. There is no incentive for achievement. They are too far away from the West to pick up TV signals to see another way of life and make comparisons."

Returning home to the West through East Berlin, Charles and John were walking to the Friedrich Strasse crossing point when two teenage girls called out to them.

"Any room in those suitcases for us?"

"Sorry."

"What a pity," said the girls.

Charles's absences from Berlin were becoming longer and longer. The agents who booked the duo's engagements and their individual engagements were in West Germany. We considered a move to Bavaria. Charles started looking for a house in Munich while I quietly began to clear out cupboards. We were not going to tell the children of our plans until we knew more.

West Berlin began to look different somehow. The idea of imminent departure played games with my perception. The city became more beautiful and even more fascinating. I was a tourist again, carefully planning excursions for the family.

I would introduce the children to some ancient history by taking them to the Pergamon Museum in East Berlin. We telephoned Detlev and Ursula and told them we were coming over to the East. On the appointed day, I called to say we were on our way.

Phone conversations with friends in East Berlin were never chatty and flippant. You didn't say, ""Hi there! What's new, and how's Peter's cold?"Or, "Wasn't that a terrific hailstorm we had last night?" Somehow, even though you had nothing whatsoever to hide, you felt you should watch your words. Someone might have been listening, so you got to the point.

"We're leaving now. We'll be crossing the checkpoint in about twenty minutes."

I slammed down the receiver and complained, "I feel like I'm taking part in a spy thriller. For crying out loud, we're only going to see a museum and visit friends. Where's the crime in that?"

Charles looked at me without answering. His eyes said: That's the way it is—in Berlin.

I remembered to bring along my porcelain coffee filter holder and some rolls of aluminum foil.

The Pergamon Museum housed the restored temple, the parade route, and the Istar Gate of ancient Babylon. The signs read 580 v.u.Z. (Vor unsere Zeit), that is, before our time, not before

Christ as such ancient history museum displays were dated in the West.

Ursula admitted that she had not been to the Pergamon Museum in fifteen years, not since she had been a schoolgirl . The Pergamon was a twenty-minute walk from the Konrads' apartment. I told her not to feel bad; I hadn't seen old Nefertiti over in the West for at least five years.

Detlev was amused at my tourist behavior, for I was carrying around a rented tape player, which ordered me around the museum in English, describing in my ear what I was seeing.

When Peter and Scott met again, they giggled their delight. They played hide-and-seek among the ancient monoliths. They sat on the bottom step of the 2,500-year-old altar, grinning at each other, oblivious to ancient history and international grand larceny, the actual stealing of Babylonian edifices, stone for stone, and transporting them to Germany.

Later that afternoon, Lynne and I went shopping with Ursula. Jens needed jeans. We went to three different stores, but we could not find jeans in his size. Each time Ursula lined up patiently, only to hear that they were out of that size. Maybe in four months, maybe six, they would receive new supplies.

Blue denims had become so popular in the German Democratic Republic (East Germany) that the government had started producing their own brand of jeans. They were known among the youth as Honecker Hot Pants, named after Eric Honecker, the first secretary of the Socialist Unity Party. One pair sold for about one third of an average worker's monthly wage. Nevertheless, everywhere we looked, we saw young people wearing jeans.

I wondered how I could get a pair of boy's jeans, size fourteen, over to the East. In my mind's eye, I could see them hanging in abundance in any one of the department stores just on the other side of town.

One week before, two brothers had flown their single-engine plane from East Germany and had landed safely in West Berlin's

British Gatow Airfield. But I knew of no small plane flying east-ward that might bring to Ursula a pair of boy's jeans.

We started back to the Konrads' apartment. We were walking along Unter den Linden toward Alexander Platz. At one corner, I looked down a side street. Silhouetted against the evening sky was a winged horse, perched on a corner of a majestic old building.

"Ursula, what is that building?"

"That is the old Schauspielhaus. It is being restored. They will have halls for concerts and plays. That whole area used to be called the Gendarmenmarkt, but now it is called Platz der Akademie. Someday it will be the most beautiful of all centers of culture," said Ursula. She seemed to be reciting something she had read.

Old drawings that I had seen of Berlin often depicted the Gendarmenmarkt, but I had never been able to find it on an up-to-date map. Now I understood why.

We were warming ourselves with coffee, anticipating our re-turn journey through the barricades once more to our home in the West, when Ursula asked shyly, "We watch a lot of your television. I've counted five different kinds of soap that are sold in the West. Do you really have five different soaps?"

"Soap for washing clothes?" I asked. She nodded, her eyes studying my face intently.

"Oh, at least five, probably more."

"It's not just Western propaganda then? We've been told it's just propaganda," she said.

"These different soap manufacturers are competing for buy-ers," I tried to explain.

We were standing at her bedroom window. Looking out over the rooftops of East Berlin and across the Wall, we could see high-rise apartment buildings in the West.

"We have *one* soap powder here. There is no competition." Her voice was soft and sad.

I asked myself, "Is this the 'enemy' side? Is this depressing, rundown country really a threat to our way of life? If this country is enemy, then where is the threat to 'our side'?"

The United States was maintaining a strong defense system against this? I imagined myself writing a letter to the president of the United States. "Dear Mr. President: The Communist world is falling apart. We have nothing to fear." Then I thought, hold on, if the opponent is weak, wouldn't that make a mockery of all the military hardware, the vast military organization, all those fine upstanding military officers? Oh.

I thought about the pictures of different soaps that Ursula had counted. I knew she had begun to wonder not only about soap, but also about coffee and chocolate and chewing gum, and all the other products advertised on West German television. The border guards could confiscate printed material, but there was no stopping the electronic beams carrying images and stories of a Western way of life. No Wall could block screenfuls of cars and cigarettes and houses and shoes. And what about *Little House on the Prairie,* that morality play of early America? Thoughts and ideas were flying over the Wall of reinforced concrete that had been built to last 100 years. And surely our visits and the visits of thousands of relatives from the West were an undermining force: people talking to people, relaying a truth that could not be silenced.

And there was truth in history as well. Every springtime in West Berlin, radio and television programs, newspapers and magazines were filled with items about history. Lest we forget what some of us could only have learned through books, pictures, and the accounts of older people, we would always be reminded that in the spring of 1949 the Berlin Blockade had been lifted.

The American general, Lucius D. Clay, who had organized the airlift that kept Berlin supplied with food and medicine, died on April 16, 1978. His death caused a spate of film documentary reruns on the evening news programs and special tributes. The next day, I was driving down Clayallee, the wide boulevard named after him, speeding a little toward my friend Meg's house, where we were to meet with Nancy, another American friend, for an excursion to Steinstuecken, a piece of West Berlin real estate nestled quirkily inside East Berlin. Steinstuecken was a part of West Berlin, but the two were attached only by a one-mile road, bordered on either side by the Wall and East German territory. It was a kind of internesting puzzle, like those famous German compound sentences. Let's see . . . where are the verbs?

After we gathered, we climbed into one car for the quick drive through midmorning traffic, a turn left off Koenigsallee, and left again under the S-Bahn tracks. Then we were alone on the new road, away from the hustle and bustle of the rest of West Berlin.

The houses in Steinstuecken were once Prussian country houses, and they reminded me of gingerbread houses. Across a footbridge was a playground and two helicopter blades, standing vertically. The blades formed a monument to the helicopter pilots who brought food and medical necessities to this little enclave after it had been completely cut off from the city when the Wall was built in 1961, but before the connecting road was re-opened in 1972.

"By the way, Lucius Clay died last night," announced Nancy.

"Who? Cassius Clay?" asked Meg.

"No, Lucius, Lucius, you know, Clayallee. I expect the flags will be flying at half mast today."

The next evening, my usually fastidiously punctual English conversation student arrived a little late, apologizing, "I had to drop my husband off at the America House. He wanted to sign in the book for General Clay."

"He wanted to send his condolences," I said slowly.

"Yes, he wanted to send his condolences."

"Were many people there?"

"Quite a crowd. All old people. The ones who remember."

I wondered how long it would be before no one was left who remembered General Clay and the airlift. Now the Wall, that was built to last 100 years. People would remember the Wall.

On Whitsuntide Monday 1978, the weather was 100% soggy. Charles, Lynne, Scott, and I set out for a drive to the lakes of West Berlin. But thousands of Berlin motorists and visitors from out of town had the same idea. In the pouring rain, we inched forward, bumper to bumper. We finally reached Glienicke Bridge, which connects West Berlin to Potsdam. Glienicke Bridge, or Freedom Bridge, was where political prisoners from both sides of the Cold War were swapped like human pawns in a giant game of chess. Glienicke Bridge marked the edge of our world, our city of West Berlin.

We parked the car and went to the banks of the Havel and looked across the water in the direction of Potsdam. But Potsdam was shrouded in heavy mist and hardly visible. We watched the cruise ships sail up to the bridge, then turn around. We pointed and identified the East German border guards whose patrol boats plied the waters, always careful to navigate on the eastern side of the line of buoys marking the border. And we knew that those guards, like all East German border guards, were under orders to shoot to kill anyone trying to cross from East to West. We reminded ourselves of this, and, heavy with the awareness of it all, we returned to our car and inched our way back toward the center of town.

That's what was different about a simple family excursion in West Berlin. Politics and history bore down on you at every turn. And you were aware of it. You always felt a heightened sense of risk. After all, five Russian military divisions were positioned within twenty miles of the city. And some West Berliners still kept suitcases packed, ready for swift evacuation. Meanwhile Charles and I were making our own quiet preparations to leave the city. Munich would be a new experience. And anyway, sooner or later, we surely would be returning to the States. For now, my job was to enjoy Berlin, both sides of it.

Ice-cream parlors called Old San Francisco and boasting thirty-four flavors had sprung up in West Berlin. We thought for sure we would hit a crowd when we decided to go to one of them on that rainy Whitsuntide Monday. But Old San Francisco on the Kurfürstendamm, West Berlin's main thoroughfare, wasn't crowded at all.

Long mirrors hung on opposing walls, and if we looked intently into one, we could see our images reflected a multitude of times, stretching far back into the dimmer recesses of the mirrors. Old San Francisco, something from the New World, had been brought as a new idea to the Old World. The old and the new moving back and forth as do the images in opposing mirrors. Old San Francisco, with its hot fudge sundaes (pronounced "Hot Fatsch" the menu explained) had established itself all over West Berlin, which had risen from the ashes of a dreadful war and was hopefully awaiting, despite its separation from West Germany, the boom and huge prosperity enjoyed there.

From Old San Francisco, we went into the Ku-damm Karree, an indoor shopping area. On this holiday, the shops were closed, but the flea market was open. Here, within the bowels of a city building, pipes and insulation lay bare in unfinished walls. The Ku-damm Karree had been planned as a complex of small shops and offices, but one section had yet to attract renters, financial flow had ceased, and construction could not be completed. For the time being, it was a flea market.

I thought of the scavengers picking their way through the piles of discarded items along our street during the Junk Days when we had cleared out our pantry, and I wondered if someone might be paying money for something I had thrown away.

We were about to leave this indoor shopping space when the sound and swinging beat of jazz music pulled us in another direction. A lilting mezzo-soprano was singing a melody I knew so well, although camouflaged now by a new rhythm. What was that tune?

We came to an open space between two shops and a restaurant, where a stage had been erected. Our friend Dorothy was singing *Just a Closer Walk with Thee*. A crowd was gathering to listen, and they began to sway to the beat.

Dorothy, an American singer, had come to Germany longer ago than even we. A fun-loving, teasing soul, she always kept you guessing about how long she had been in Germany and how old she was. As the song ended, we cheered and clapped with the audience, then made our way to the rainy outside once more.

In May 1978, Charles was performing at the Gaertner Platz Theater in Munich. He had registered our name and desired house size with one of the largest and most reputable real-estate agencies in Munich. One evening Charles telephoned. He was excited. "Honey, I've found our new house!"

"Wonderful."

"It is just two subway stations from the American school. The people who live there now were very nice. They showed me through the house. There is a shopping area within walking distance. And, oh honey, there's a backyard! I can have my little vegetable garden."

Was that a yearning in his voice for a vegetable garden? I had no idea that it was so important to him. The house owner was out of town but would return in three days. It wasn't worth Charles's flying back to Berlin; he'd just wait in Munich.

"Well?" I said when Charles telephoned again. I had just spent three days clearing out closets.

"Well, I talked to the house owner."

"And?"

"She asked some pretty funny questions."

"Like what?"

"She wanted to know whether my wife was a good housekeeper and whether you could keep the place clean. I said you were a very good housekeeper."

"That was a lie," I said.

"She wanted to know whether I was sure I would be happy in the neighborhood. I said I'd lived in Germany for seventeen years and had always got along with the neighbors. Then she wanted to know whether you were German, and when I told her you were Filipino she said, 'Oh, another colored person.' "

"She said she is a professor at the Musik Hochschule and really wants to help a fellow musician, but now she's decided to sell, not rent. Could I afford 150,000 West marks to buy the house? I said no. She said she was sorry then.

"I called the rental agency immediately. They were very embarrassed. They had no record of her ever saying she wanted to sell the house."

"Surely that is not the only house for rent in all of Munich," I tried to make light of it, but there was a controlled raspiness in his voice now that I had never heard before.

"I know," he said. "We'll just keep looking."

I thought of Charles those many years before, standing at a newspaper kiosk in Zehlendorf, and of the Berlinerin who pointed to Charles, then to herself, and to the little white card that said "*Zimmer Frei.*" When we moved to Munich would we not be welcomed? Would we be leaving one kind of wall to experience the wall of racism?

The question turned out to be moot for the time being, for a steady stream of engagements filled summer 1978, and the calendar looked busy and rosy for the fall. In addition, negotiations were underway for work in (gasp!) West Berlin. Would I actually have my husband home and working? Was there no end to our good fortune?

After eight years in our spacious but dreary Halensee apartment, we could now afford to have it painted and wallpapered. It had not seen a new coat of paint in years.

We were not moving away from the city after all. Instead, we seemed to be digging in more deeply. After contracting a housepainting firm, we scheduled the estimated three weeks' work on the apartment to coincide with our holiday in Italy. Why not have the painters paint while we sunbathed on the Riviera?

A spring season of long wet weeks had followed a mild winter, and summer 1978 seemed destined to continue cool and rainy. So we joined the thousands of sun-starved Northern Europeans from Scandinavia, Germany, and Holland, and headed south.

After we had been on the southern side of the Brenner Pass for thirty minutes, the curtain of rain clouds lifted. The sun was blinding. For the first time in months, it was warm enough to take off our sweaters.

The Italian Riviera was jam-packed with people. Prices were outrageous. But who cared? The sun was shining!

While lying on my allotted piece of sand, I imagined the painters in our apartment back in Berlin painting away, bringing to light the minor league palace that surely lay beneath the cracked and yellowing wallpaper.

"I'm glad you telephoned," said our neighbor when we called three weeks later to say we would be returning the next evening. "I'll have to make a path for you at least from the front door to your beds. No, they haven't finished. They've hardly started."

Hardly started? What had the painters been doing for the past three weeks?

We arrived home after midnight and crawled wearily into bed after the long drive. At 7:00 the next morning, the doorbell rang, and one painter arrived. By 9:00, he had changed into his work clothes and was having breakfast. For two hours he had done nothing. Then a second workman joined him.

We checked the progress they had made in twenty-one days. The wallpaper in two rooms had been stripped. The paint on window frames and doors in one room had been burned off. That was all.

For the next three and a half weeks, we let in the painters every morning, then confined ourselves to the rooms where they were not working. We ate out often. The summer season dragged on, showery and cool. We seemed to spend most of our time moving piles of one room's contents into another room. I could never remember where anything was.

The kitchen was being painted when a salesman from a firm selling built-in cabinets came calling. I was searching for Scott's bathing trunks; a new kitchen was the furthest thing from my mind.

"Isn't it a bit extravagant?" I asked Charles.

"Oh, go on, you deserve a new kitchen. Anyway, look at the work lined up for the fall," he urged.

On a day when the sun almost shone, the painters finished. The last ladder had just been hauled out of sight, and I was taking out a can of garbage when Frau Schreiber, the white-haired Oma in the ground floor apartment, called out the window. "Frau Williams! Frau Williams, congratulations on your new kitchen!" She'd been watching the Williams new kitchen show the entire time.

What is it about a new kitchen that spells permanence? Cooking and cleaning chores were easier now that the children were old enough to help. I cultivated my ineptitude at housework knowingly, always allowing Charles to take over whenever he was home. When he cleaned floors or windows or stoves, they stayed clean much longer. And he cooked with creative flair.

"After all," Charles would boast, "I came from a long line of maids."

Had we moved to Munich, we would have put the children in the American schools there. Now that we were not moving, we decided to transfer the children from the bilingual German-American John F. Kennedy School to the American schools for Department of Defense dependents. I was not satisfied with the bilingual school and did not think it would give our children an adequate preparation for further studies in the United States. I was hearing stories of students completing high school at the bilingual school, only to flunk American college entrance exams because their English was weak. An all-English school would help our children succeed in an American university.

When the school year began, Lynne auditioned as a flute player and was accepted into the Berlin American High School intermediate band.

Scott entered fifth grade at the Thomas A. Roberts Elementary School.

The following spring, the intermediate band performed at the Tempelhof Open House, and although it rained and rained, we joined the crowds at the American military airfield in Tempelhof to look at the planes on display and hear the band perform. Later we took Scott and Lynne to the U.S. air base's most famous aircraft. It was known as the "candy bomber" because during the Berlin Airlift in 1948 and 1949, it was one of the planes that had dropped chocolate and other candy to West Berlin's children.

West Berlin continually presented opportunities like this for parents to explain history to their children. We told Lynne and Scott that the Airlift was the Western Allies' response to the Soviet Blockade of Berlin, and the Blockade was the Soviets' reaction to the creation of the Federal Republic of Germany and the West German deutsche mark.

Soviet occupying forces had blockaded the part of Berlin held by the Western Allies by stopping the flow of land traffic to and from the city. During the ensuing Airlift that kept the city supplied with food and medicine, candy was dropped to Berlin children, still playing amid the heaps of wartime rubble.

As I ended my history lesson, I could hear other parents around us. "We were so happy to see chocolate falling from the sky. We had nothing then. Nowhere to play. Everything was still in ruins."

Now, thirty years after the Blockade and Airlift, Berliners and we *Wahlberliners* watched the skies once more as two helicopters, one spewing forth red smoke, one spewing forth green smoke, flew overhead. My thoughts reached across town and over the Wall to the East, where I hoped Jens was watching from his rooftop lookout in that other world on the other side of the Wall.

In the second week of October, the phone rang four fateful times. One after another, four well-paying jobs were suddenly canceled.

My tummy elevator plummeted. Sometimes one has a headache, but doesn't know it until it is gone. That tummy elevator had been a constant companion of mine through our early Berlin years. Only now, on its return, did I realize that it had been absent for a while. We had reveled in temporary prosperity, but now that prosperity was threatened.

Since Charles and John had received a tentative offer for work at the Friedrichstadtpalast in East Berlin, beginning in January, they crossed the border to reconfirm the offer. An artist had just canceled unexpectedly, said the people in East Berlin's largest variety theater, would they mind beginning work immediately?

Right away, Charles and John began to work. And right away, they began to earn well, unbelievably well. The only hitch was that their wages were paid in East German marks. Never mind, I thought, the East Berliners all spend their money in East Berlin. We could, too.

We led busy lives. In the daily routine of shopping, cooking, cleaning, and chauffeuring children around to extracurricular activities, it was not easy to schedule in a time to cross a border, but there it sat, marking the edge of our world, faking accessibility. Oh, we never really wanted to admit it—crossing over was such a hassle. Why would one purposely plan unpleasantness into a day? We weren't fueling the fire of a romance. We weren't going over to visit a friend in hospital. We were going to the East to spend money.

A six-week run of nightly engagements seemed such a long time. Charles was going over every day, buying this and that—inconsequential things, at first.

At the beginning of the third week, he said, "I saw a nice mink coat over there. It was your size."

"What would I do with a mink?" I asked.

"Wear it."

I hesitated. A mink coat wasn't just a fur coat. It was a status symbol. It signified a style of life I had chosen to defy. I had turned away from the privileged life of a diplomat's daughter. I wanted my own adventure.

"Look, honey, I could not afford a mink for you here in the West," Charles urged.

At that moment, I was in the kitchen peeling potatoes. I raised my eyes from my busy hands and regarded an invisible space of thought on the wall straight ahead. I thought of how far this man had come. Beneath this hardworking artist whose smile and positive energy could win the hearts of audiences, there lived a little boy from Haynesville, a tiny town in northern Louisiana. For a moment, I saw a barefoot child running down a dusty road, grinning, excited, happy. He was almost always happy, this man that I loved so much, happy and sure that the gods would always be on his side. This man deserved to have a wife who wore a mink coat, a coat he was able to buy for her.

"Okay, buy it," I said.

Meanwhile our deutsche-mark resources were dwindling fast, and we were not sure how we would pay next month's rent. In the middle of the week, I bought hamburger meat and, lacing it with rolled oats, made a large meatloaf that was to last for three dinners. That evening, Charles brought home the mink.

Suddenly, there were only ten days left before the East Berlin engagement was over, and we'd hardly made a dent in our accumulated East German soft, soft currency. The largest denomination in East German currency was 100 marks. Whenever we went shopping, we had to haul around thousands of marks in bulky bills. It was almost obscene.

Over there, down the street in East Berlin, across the border, there was another country. Customs duty was charged on all goods bought in East Berlin and carried over into West Berlin, unless the buyer was employed in the East or unless the buyer belonged to one of the occupying Western forces.

During the length of Charles's contract in East Berlin, he could buy goods and bring them home duty free. This privilege was not extended to me. Carrying purchases, I would always have to cross back into the West with Charles. And time was running out.

Charles's partner, John, was broad shouldered and powerfully built. He was having the time of his life buying clothes, buying clothes, buying clothes. They didn't have clothes to fit Charles's slighter frame. In utter frustration, Charles came home one day with eight umbrellas. "Two for each of us. At least I could buy umbrellas!" he hollered. "And there weren't any long lines for umbrellas!"

"Lines?" Oh, of course, the lines. I remembered Ursula lining up patiently again and again to buy a pair of jeans.

When only one week remained of Charles's East Berlin engagement, he took me to the exclusive ladies' shops on Unter den Linden, East Berlin's most famous avenue. The shops opened at 10:00 *A.M.*

For the first hour I had a blast. If I liked something, and it fit, I bought it and asked how much later. It was fun!

By 11:00 A.M., lines had started forming at all the counters. Many in the crowd were from Eastern Bloc countries. I recognized the Russian officers' uniforms, but I could not distinguish one Slavic tongue from another.

At each counter you could reckon on a wait of at least ten minutes as the line moved slowly forward. It was close to Christmas, and people wanted to buy. Often, however, after waiting in line, they'd decide the item was too expensive after all.

I stood in line at the leather-goods counter. I observed what others were buying. One small change purse was carefully inspected for quality. It cost thirty marks. Should one splurge? One silk scarf cost sixty marks. I thought of what the average East Berliners earned. For them, these prices were exorbitant.

We were not allowed to bring East money over to the West. It wouldn't even have been worthwhile smuggling currency over in our shoes because its exchange value was four or five East marks for one West mark. That crime really didn't pay.

The line at the leather-goods counter shuffled forward. Then it was my turn. I'll have that purse there, please. And that little one over there and four of those scarves. Oh, yes, and three billfolds, please. Why not throw in that cute little cosmetic purse just for fun? As I paid for my purchases, I could feel those still in line staring at me. I wanted to pin a declaration on my back that said:

"Listen people, it's like this. I'm not what it looks like. I'm not a rich capitalist, exploiting you. This is your currency I'm spending, see. I'm doing my best to plow it back into your economy because I have to. Understand?"

I turned from the cash register and started for the door. Their eyes stung me. It was a cold stare that made me squirm. No, they didn't understand. How could they?

At 9:00 the next morning, Charles took me to the Centrum department store and then went off to check into record players. Only the Centrum's gift-shop section was open.

Did they have any Christmas tablecloths? Christmas napkins? How about Christmas decorations? Christmas wall hangings? No, no, no. All the time the answer was no.

I wanted to ask, by the way, have you ever heard of Christmas? I had thousands of marks jammed into my purse and pockets, and there seemed to be nothing to buy.

I spied a pile of what I thought were boxes of Christmas-tree candles. Ah, I could supply our family and Tante Susi's family, all of our friends, and neighbors with Christmas-tree candles for years and years.

"I'd like some Christmas-tree candles," I told the salesperson.

"Sorry, we're all sold out."

At 9:40 A.M., I walked slowly across Alexander Platz to the Kleine Centrum department store. The doors were to open in twenty minutes, and a crowd was forming fast. I thought of how often I had driven to Wilmersdorfer Strasse in West Berlin in time for the department stores to open at 9:00, how often I'd made my purchases and been back home at 10:30. No crowds, no lines.

Four large, fully stocked department stores stood along Wilmersdorfer Strasse, in Wilmersdorf, one of twelve districts in the western part of the city. Ka-De-We, the Kaufhaus des Westens, Europe's second largest department store, second only to Paris's Au Printemps, was located at one end of the Kurfuerstendamm. Each of West Berlin's districts had an abundance of stores and goods.

East Berlin had its Centrum.

The doors opened, and I was swept in with the crowd. Immediately, lines formed at counters. I was becoming sick and tired of lines. Over in the corner there was a counter without a line. I hurried over to it.

"I'll take ten, please!" I panted.

"Ten of what?"

"It doesn't matter. I'll take ten of whatever you're selling." The saleswoman looked at me as though I were from outer space.

Scott needed gym shoes. I lined up for the escalator (yes, there were lines for the escalators) and went to the sports department. They were out of Scott's shoe size. I did, however, succeed in buying a pretty serving bowl and winter coats for the children. Both coats were in beige, an easily soiled color and thus impractical for children's wear. They only came in beige: racks and racks of children's coats, all sizes but all beige.

Once again I wondered This is our enemy? We have to defend our way of life—against *this*? How could the scarcities of this lopsided economy be a threat? Racks and racks of beige children's coats. Honestly.

By now, the lines everywhere were formidable. I lined up patiently at every floor's escalator and made my way slowly to the outside, vowing never to return to the Centrum.

Charles and I were to meet at the camera shop. The line there was only five people long.

"I'd like a camera, please."

"Well—what *kind* would you *like*?" the salesperson snapped.

I was running out of time and patience. I snapped back, "What is your *best* camera?"

With a subservience plucked from the ether, she smiled widely and proceeded to demonstrate the many virtues of the Praktica MTL3, the best camera the German Democratic Republic had to offer—indeed, one of the best cameras in the world. I bought a flash attachment to go with it. It was the only model they had for sale.

Having lots and lots of money and little choice of things to buy was no fun at all. Later, I shared a meal with one of the ballet dancers from the theater. She offered to help me find things to buy next time I came across to shop.

"I'd like some of those little wooden angels or some music boxes," I told her.

"It's very hard to get those. They are mostly made for export," she said.

The woman at the next table overheard our conversation. "They are at my place," she called out, grinning.

"And where is your place?" I asked.

"In Frankfurt am Main in West Germany. I own a gift shop there."

That evening I surveyed my purchases: a serving bowl, which I could have bought in the West for half the price at the exchange rate of one West mark to one East mark; coats for the children, that was good; one very good camera and one flash attachment; ten erasers; ten bottles of glue; ten pencils; ten packages of envelopes; ten drawing pads; ten packets of rubber bands.

Our neighbor, a photographer, congratulated me on the purchase of a very good camera but advised me to return the flash. It was not a good model. I should try to get my money back or exchange it for a telescopic lens attachment.

Crossing the border was beginning to take its toll. I simply couldn't face going over again for the next two days. Charles had a pass, stating that he was professionally employed in the East, and while under contract there he was allowed to cross the border visa free. Each time I crossed over, I had to buy a visa for five deutsche marks, and we were required to exchange six and a half deutsche marks into East marks.

Each time there was a wait—ten minutes, thirty minutes. No matter how you looked at it, you were at the mercy of the mood of the guard on duty. If he didn't like the look of you, if he didn't like the shape of your eyebrows, he could detain you. He could search you. He could make you strip. If you were a woman, he could have you examined gynecologically. He could make you take your car apart and put it back together again. All this was within his range of power. He knew it, and you knew it, too.

Passports were examined four times by uniformed men who checked to see that the passport in their hands said the right things about you. While they checked, I was thinking: Yes, I'm me. I

know I'm me. Those who love me know it. How dare you, all of
you, check me! I'm me, and God knows it, too. You four guys
don't even matter. But, of course, I didn't tell them that. Should I
rob them of their job? They were border police. Who knew how
many weeks and months of what kind of intensive training they
had gone through to learn their skills?

At each of four control points, I handed over my papers and
waited. Is every *i* dotted correctly and every *t* crossed? Are my
eyes smiling correctly, or are they crossed? Will you let me cross
this border that you have been trained to guard? Will you? Well,
will you? Who said you should set up this border, anyway? Are
you my enemy? Have I committed a crime against you or anyone? If so, what crime? Tell me, so I can repent and make amends.
I have a number on my passport. You check to see that the number I have written on the piece of paper is the same as the number on the passport. In kindergarten I was champion at copying
down numbers. This is my number. It is another name for me,
like a prisoner's number, a criminal's number. Did my number
commit a crime? You are a human and so am I. I trust someone
must have been your mother. I have a mother, too. We share this
earth. We breathe the same air. What man-made idea separates
us now?

"I can't take another border crossing," I told Charles on Monday.

"We don't have much time," he said. "But maybe today we
can buy that new kitchen table we've been promising ourselves."

Our new kitchen cupboards had been installed for months,
but we still had not purchased the table and chairs we had long
ago picked out from the IKEA catalog.

IKEA was a well-known name in West Germany, and West
Berlin. IKEA was a name that always appeared beside the words
"the impossible furniture house from Sweden" on posters, in newspaper and magazine ads. IKEA was a furniture company that produced Scandinavian designed furniture at reasonable prices. We
had been studying IKEA catalogs for the past two years. Terrific

bargains. We chose a table called Bromma. It cost seventy-four deutsche marks.

Charles had our new table upside down on the kitchen floor and was attaching the legs when he called out to me, "There's a stamp on the underneath side of our new table. You know what it says?"

I came into the kitchen. "What?"

"Made in GDR, the German Democratic Republic."

I couldn't believe my eyes. The more I thought about it, the angrier I got. "Inexpensive furniture of this quality is not available over there," I said.

"They have shortages of everything there," said Charles. "One stagehand at Friedrichstadtpalast told me this joke. A shopper goes to the Centrum department store and asks, 'Do you have any white paint?' The salesperson says, 'No, in this department we are out of curtains. Go upstairs, that's where they are out of white paint.' " A year before, I would not have gotten this joke, but now I laughed long and loud.

Charles continued, "The man who told me that joke often accompanies me to the door when I leave the theater. There's something sad about him. Sort of, I don't know, fragmented. He told me he used to live in an apartment on the corner of Kurfuerstendamm and Schlüterstrasse."

"What a terrific location. Right in the center of town," I said.

"But when the Wall went up he had to decide whether to live in the East or the West. Jobs were scarce then, so he decided to stay in the East," said Charles.

I remembered the secretary at the U.S. Mission who had chosen to stay with her job in the American Sector, and I wondered what choice, job or apartment, I would have made.

The whole East-West nonsense was making my head mushy. It made me angry. It made me laugh. It made me sad. And it was pushing me, the ardent nonmaterialist, into rapacious consumerism in a Socialist state. But I had to be practical. There was still a mountain of East German money we needed to spend, and I had to exchange the flash attachment.

On Thursday, two days before Charles's last performance at Friedrichstadtpalast, we crossed the border at 8:00 A.M. Between 9 and 10, we bought groceries. I had become hardened; I no longer cared how the other housewives in the lines judged me. I knew what I had to do.

The woman in the meat line in front of me had red-raw dishpan hands. She couldn't make up her mind whether she wanted a pound of stewing beef or two small pork chops. Apparently, her budget didn't stretch to buying both.

Oh, sister, I've been there. I know what that's like. She bought the chops.

Our turn. We bought two kilos each of several kinds of meat in the showcase, and twenty pork chops and hurried away without looking back. At other counters we bought two cases of champagne, a dozen jars of caviar, ten pounds of cheese, three frozen chickens, and two frozen ducks.

As we lined up to check out, a radio loudspeaker squawked overhead. East German radio news was reporting widespread unemployment, homelessness, and unrest in the decadent United States of America. A sign above the cashier's head told us she was an apprentice being trained by the Socialist Party. In the East, they were always proud to demonstrate how there was no unemployment, that everyone had a job.

The young cashier's mouth gaped as we checked through the contents of our grocery baskets. Our purchases equaled her month's salary.

We decided that the children should have a telescope to gaze at the stars. While I stood in line at the camera counter to exchange the flash attachment, Charles went next door to buy the telescope.

I was sixth in my line, but the line was moving forward quickly, for two customers in front of me asked about flash attachments and were told that flash attachments were sold out. No model of any kind was available.

My turn. The salesperson, the same smiling, subservient one from Monday, was unmoving and cold. No, no return, no refund, no exchange. None of my alternative suggestions was possible.

"You can try to get rid of it over there." She waved haughtily toward the right. I looked right. Above a door a sign said "*Gelegenheiten*" (Bargains). It was the secondhand buying and selling counter.

I lined up again. When I was second in line, the man behind me spoke over my head to the salesperson, "I just have a question. Do you have any flash attachments of any kind?" The salesperson shook his head.

I turned around. "What kind are you looking for? I have one right here."

We left the line together and retreated to a far corner. "See? I bought it on Monday. I only want what I paid for it. Here's the guarantee and everything."

He was a very thin man. He started chuckling. He opened his wallet and counted out fifty marks. He needed another twenty-five marks. He searched for more money in all of his other pockets. His hands were trembling. Slowly, I realized that from Monday to this Thursday all flash attachments in East Berlin had been sold out.

"Please wait right here," he said desperately. "I'll bring you the rest of the money in just a little while."

"I'll be next door where the telescopes are. My husband is in there. I'll meet you in thirty minutes, and then I'm afraid I can't wait any longer," I told him. We synchronized watches.

"You'll get your money, I promise." He dashed away.

Next door where they sold telescopes, I found Charles. He was tenth in line, and he looked utterly disgusted. I told him what had just transpired. Charles was in a hurry, "We'll have to forget the telescope. I need to buy the toolbox. I don't think there will be a line for toolboxes. I'll meet you at the bookstore at 1:00 P.M."

The trembling thin man returned. He had not been successful in cashing a check, but he'd been told you could cash checks on the top floor of the Centrum.

Oh no, I groaned inwardly, not the Centrum. We started to cross Alexander Platz. Should I be generous and say, "Look mister, my husband is earning gobs of your money, see? Why not keep your twenty-five marks? I've got this problem of time."

No, these people had pride, I couldn't do that. Maybe I could suggest that he leave twenty-five marks at the theater whenever he got it together. No, I didn't like that plan either. The run of Charles's engagement was ending. How soon would we be back? Anyway, we were now entering the Centrum. Oh, horrors.

Up the escalator to the bank on the top floor. Four teller windows were open. Each had a line fifteen people long. "I'll wait for you there." I retreated to a chair against the wall several yards away.

The top floor of the Centrum was just as crowded as every other floor. I watched the people lining up for the descending escalators. I watched the people move patiently forward in the bank teller lines.

On the other side of the escalator there was yet another line. My eyes followed it to its head. A lone saleswoman stood there, wearing a tightly fitting dress. She was blond and quite obese, and everything about her spoke of fullness, bulging abundance, and jollity, a veritable female Santa Claus. She towered over a tiny cash register, which she rang again and again. She was selling coconuts.

My thin man returned. He wasn't trembling any more. He gave me the money, I handed him the flash, and we lined up for the escalator. As we started our descent, I counted the money. Thirty marks.

"I owe you five." I reached for my purse.

"No, please. It's all right." He gave me a precious little hug. He was very, very contented with himself. I was trying hard to spend money, and now I'd made a profit. Great.

That afternoon I looked at Christmas trees for sale. How inexpensive they were! They were in a space under an elevated portion of the S-Bahn, the East Berlin city railroad. A fir tree, my height (five foot) was only two and a half East marks. But the trees were not displayed neatly or set on little stands. They were piled high, lying on their sides, their stumps jutting out at you like rifles through a fortress wall.

You had to yank one free from the pile to try to assess its symmetry in the gathering darkness while the wind blew snow in your face and the S-Bahn rumbled overhead, sending gritty specks of dust into your eyes. I ended up buying the only fir tree I was able to liberate from the stack.

With no enthusiasm at all, I went shopping one last time on the day of Charles's final performance at the Friedrichstadtpalast. The winds were icy and the snowfall heavy. But my new fur coat was warm and my boots fur-lined and dry. I stood in a few lines if they were not too long and bought things I didn't need.

That evening, Charles moved about the stage with great gusto, singing in German *Viel Zu Heiss* (*Too Darn Hot.*) Charles and John sang their duet—"*Ein Freund, Ein Guter Freund, das ist der Schönste, daß es gibt auf der Welt*"—charming the audience of East Germans. Present also were Russian army officers in dress uniform. They belonged to the occupation forces of the East, still officially an ally of the United States, France, and Britain, allies against the German enemy, now vanquished.

And who indeed was that vanquished enemy? Surely it couldn't be Tante Susi, Onkel Werner, or Mama in Augsburg? What about the teachers at the St. Michaelsheim, who taught my children music, pottery, batik, even photography? What about Ursula in the East, and the artists on stage with Charles at the Friedrichstadtpalast?

"Ein Freund bleibt immer Freund, auch wenn die ganze Welt zusammen fällt . . . [A friend is always a friend, even if the whole world collapses . . .]," sang Charles and John that night, and as every night before, the audience began clapping to the beat. But in 1978, who was friend and who was foe? I could not tell. I could not pull apart the internesting clauses and translate them into something clear, as I sat in the Friedrichstadtpalast in East Berlin, the capital city of the most successful Socialist country of the Warsaw Pact.

During the finale that evening, each ballerina presented Charles and John with a pink carnation. Each male dancer shook their hands. The carnations and handshakes said thank you. Thank you for coming over to our side, since we can't go over to yours. Thank you for sharing your laughter, your friendship, your freedom.

One week before Christmas I delivered Lynne to one Christmas party and Scott to another. I found myself alone in the Zehlendorf District in the West. The shops would not be closing for another two hours. Beside the 200-year-old church on the corner of Clayallee and Unter den Eichen, a Christmas tree salesman had set out his wares. Bright lights hung from the ancient oak tree on the corner. The Christmas trees stood in neat rows, and I could see that they were of very good quality. The price tag on a fir tree as tall as I read thirty-six deutsche marks.

I had finished my Christmas shopping, but I decided just to browse. Along Clayallee next to the church a gift shop and a toy store stood side by side. There were no crowds, no lines. The goods for sale stood row upon row in quiet abundance: pretty things, cute gifts, gag gifts; made in Taiwan, made in Japan, made in Hong Kong. The wooden miniatures of animals, flowers, and angels I recognized as products of East Germany. I walked up and down the aisles of merchandise. Here, on this side of the Wall, there was so much. So much. My temporary home was imbalanced: so much on one side; too little on the other. What was my responsibility toward all this, this city with a Wall? After all, I had chosen to come live here. I thought of that newlywed with shining eyes, seventeen years before, who had said breathlessly, "Yes, let's go to Berlin." I was not just a rootless woman without a country, I was a *Wahlberlinerin,* and I was becoming less content to just observe Berlin. I sensed that the very act of observation was in some small way causing the city to change.

CHAPTER 5

Remembering Things Past

No other portrayal of crimes committed during the Nazi regime affected attitudes in postwar Germany more deeply than the American television production of *Holocaust.* In January 1979, the third channel (Drittes Programm) in West Germany not only aired the series, but also opened the station phones immediately following each episode for questions and comments from viewers. More than 20 million West Germans watched the program. The station received more than 30,000 telephone calls.

One call came after the program had just begun. A woman in East Berlin telephoned to complain that the telecast should have been shown on the first channel, not the third. As everybody knew, said the woman from the other side of the Wall, the third channel's signal was not received clearly in the East. I wondered who this person was who was brave enough to admit over the airwaves that she watched Western television.

For four consecutive evenings, the miniseries unfolded horror upon horror before my disbelieving eyes. The knot in the pit of my stomach seemed to grow into a cannonball, and I wasn't sure I could make it through the last episode.

The next week we shared an evening meal with our good friends Sepl and Inge. No, they hadn't seen the show. They had no intention of seeing the show. "We already know about that. We don't need to be reminded."

"But how could such obvious atrocity be going on without someone doing something about it?" we wanted to know.

"You would have gone along with the crowd and kept quiet, too, Ruth," said Sepl. "And you, too, Charles, if you had been here then."

We were sitting around a fondue pot. The long, thin fork handles were pointing outward like the spokes of a wheel, each handle identified by a dot of a different color. The forks were spearing cubes of steak, and they were all together in a pot of simmering oil.

We could find no words of reply. They were our good friends. They had lavished upon us so much kindness, had helped furnish our early apartment. Like Tante Susi and Onkel Werner, they had babysat our children, loving them as their own grandchildren. They were dear people. Yet we wanted to state with certainty that we would have stood up against wickedness.

Hold on a minute, Charles and I would not have been safe enough to even take a stand. We would have had to flee immediately. Our obvious non-Germanness would not even have allowed us to assist in an underground network of resistance. Had our friends forgotten our origins? Could they somehow no longer see that we were not Caucasian? In silence, we passed the basket of baguette slices among us and reached for more condiments.

We moved on to a more neutral subject, talking about the concerts Charles was giving at the Reichskabaret that week. We planned to meet there, then go out for a drink after the show. The Reichskabaret was a small theater situated on Joachim Friedrich Strasse, twenty meters or so from the Kurfuerstendamm. Intersection. Johann Georg Strasse, an adjoining street, had not yet been turned into a cul-de-sac, and it curled around the Reichskabaret at a spot where a medical building now stands.

The following week, as I entered the theater, I noticed the Third Reich's eagle insignia above the door, worn but still discernible. Although in the company of good friends as I sat in the theater, I was aware that Charles would not have been allowed to perform there in the days of the Third Reich, when Negroes and mulattoes were prohibited from making public appearances.

Several weeks were to pass before the feelings of nausea and choking terror that *Holocaust* had provoked in me finally vanished.

It was time to stop thinking of things past, time to start plans for a future happy event. Lynne, now 13, would soon be confirmed.

Living in Germany, we were far away from our own close relatives. Charles and I wanted to include our adopted Berlin families in the celebration of Lynne's confirmation. I was on the phone with Inge, the very same hostess of the fondue evening, helping her decide on an appropriate gift for Lynne.

"How abut a Bible?"

I explained that Lynne was already receiving a Bible for her confirmation at the American Community Chapel.

"Anyway, Bibles are what brides and grooms in Germany receive at weddings," our friend admitted.

"Did you get a Bible when you got married?" I asked, hoping I might one day see a valuable old book.

"No, we got a copy of *Mein Kampf.*"

I heard my own throat utter something that was between a gag and a giggle. Then I was laughing uncontrollably. When I apologized for my laughter, the voice on the other end of the line was free of rancor.

"Go ahead and laugh. But you know we were married in 1939. At that time, receiving *Mein Kampf* as a wedding present was the usual thing."

Scott was going to a tenth birthday party right after school the next day, so that afternoon he rode his bike while I walked to the toy store to buy a present. On the store's counter, I noticed a small tube of liquid plastic with a short straw attached to it by a rubber band. Childhood memories flooded my mind. I remembered playing quietly and alone with that inflatable plastic goo, making bubble shapes of all sorts and bubble creatures.

Scott, in his sober, businesslike way had picked out a gift and was paying the man, when, overflowing with memories, I gushed,

"Oh, I remember that stuff! Isn't it wonderful how they still make it! I used to spend hours creating things with it. Didn't *you* play with it, too?"

The owner of the toy shop was perhaps three to five years my senior. He had a full head of silvering blond hair, and his thickening middle bespoke present-day good times.

"Play with toys as a child?" He lifted one side of his mouth in a twisted smile. "When I was a child, my playground was the ruins of bombed-out buildings. We had no toys. We were lucky to get enough to eat."

"That's fate, isn't it?" I said, determined not to get maudlin.

"And children nowadays," he said, as he handed Scott the motorcycle he had chosen, "have too many toys."

Scott had leaned his bicycle against a small tree outside the toy store. When we returned to it, the bicycle was gone. We reentered the store to report the bicycle's disappearance. Shaking his head and declaring it the third bicycle theft that year, the store owner came outside to look up and down the street as we had just done. Then the store owner looked down at me and said, "You know who is at fault, Frau Williams? It's the foreigners. The foreigners are responsible for all these bad things."

"Do you really think so?" I asked, trying to stand as tall as possible.

"Yes, the foreigners," he repeated.

"What's going on?" I asked Charles later. "Are we becoming invisible? First the certainty that we would have been part of the silent conspiracy during the Nazi era, and now that shopkeeper's declaring to me that the bicycle was stolen 'by foreigners.'"

"I guess the Berliners are just getting used to us," said Charles.

A few days later, Charles and I also attended a birthday party. Our invitation read: "A genuine Berliner becomes fifty." Our names had been handwritten on the card. The place of celebration would be a small hall in Kreuzberg, a district whose northern limit was the Wall, and the day would be Ascension Day, a holiday. The fiftieth birthday celebration would begin at 11:00 A.M.

Ascension Day dawned bright and unusually warm. Berliners in their summer clothes and sandals headed for the woods, parks, and beaches of their city. The roads on the way to Kreuzberg were heavy with holiday traffic.

The genuine Berliner, whose birthday it was, stood at the door of the reception hall, greeting his guests with charm and witty remarks. He was a very blond man whose ruddiness was heightened that day by soaring temperatures and humidity. There was something in his smile, a certain sparkle in his eyes, that suggested he'd just told you a joke and now he was waiting for you to get it.

An old upright piano against one wall of the reception hall supported a growing burden of flowers and presents. Across the center of the keyboard, held in place by two stout flower-filled vases, was an old flag of the NSDAP (*Nationalsozialistische Deutsche Arbeitspartei,* the National Socialist German Workers Party). It was black, white, and red, but it had no swastika. It was crumpled and heavily stained, and it caused conversation.

"Is it? Is it really?" we asked, with our insatiable foreigner's curiosity. "Is it an authentic old German flag?"

"Well, it looks like one," said the tall German guest standing uneasily beside us. He seemed to be having trouble deciding where to look. "I'm not sure, but I think showing that flag is illegal."

The noonday buffet was excellent, the champagne abundant. There were toasts and speeches and birthday congratulations.

Two hours later, our leave-taking included thanks for good food and friendship. I said, "That's an interesting flag on the piano." The guest of honor embraced us. The combination of heat, merriment, and champagne had made him ruddier than ever.

"That flag," he said proudly, "has been in my family a long time." Yes, it was a genuine old flag, he stated with pride. "What good does it do to make a new flag? Does that change people? History? If it could speak and tell us all it has seen . . . ."

The flag and the birthday host were fifty years old. As a young person he had lived through Hitler's invasion of Poland and Germany's capitulation. What happens to a person when the world about him shatters in the fragile years when dreams are born? Sometimes dashed dreams survive and lie like quiet embers, waiting. Although we were sure Nazi sentiments had long been quelled, we could not foresee what the future held for this country where we now enjoyed almost complete acceptance.

Later that afternoon, after we had returned home, the heat became oppressive. Above us, from the north, east, and south, storm clouds were converging on Berlin. A friend who had seen the approaching storm from her penthouse apartment in Reinickendorf, a district in the far north of the city, said that over Berlin that afternoon lay a brightness of sulfur yellow.

Unaware of the storm brewing above us, I prepared a leafy summer salad for my little family, and we sat on the balcony enjoying it and the twilight. Although the sky was cloud covered, those clouds were not dark and bulbous, and I could not predict that it would soon rain. Suddenly Charles announced, "It is about to storm." And big drops of rain began to splash about us.

Then there was a howl, like the screams of a thousand faraway voices racing toward us. In haste, we gathered glasses, salad plates, and forks. A piece of lettuce was picked up and flung against the balcony wall. The scream, the roar, now mingled with nearby thunder.

The rain broke through in torrents, releasing the sound of 10,000 wailing mothers watching their children suffer. The wind, carrying twigs and grit, blasted into the balcony, whipped up over the apartment house, and whistled spinning up and down through the back courtyard.

"All hands!" I shouted. Lynne and I quickly dragged balcony furniture indoors. Charles brought in the hanging geraniums, which were dancing wildly in the wind. Only Scott remained stock still within the tempest, arms flung wide, his face grinning upward into the lashing rain. After a flash of lightning and a clap of thunder, I pulled him in and closed the doors.

But the day's activities were not over yet. An hour later, with the rain still pouring, we ran to the car and drove to the Berlin

American High School, where Lynne would be playing the flute in that year's spring concert.

Contemporary American music was performed that night. The chorus sang, *I Believe in Music* and *Ease on Down the Road*. The band played *How the West Was Won* and the theme from the TV series *MASH,* while parents' home cameras whirred and flashbulbs popped. It could have been a high-school concert anywhere in America. It was, instead, in what had once been a forest, and then became part of the American Sector of a city like no other.

Alternating between the German and American languages and cultures was easy for me now. I hardly realized which language I was speaking. But one day, out of the blue, I was thrust back to my Filipino beginnings.

"Bulaklak! Bulaklak!" I called out, shouting above the clanking and grinding of the municipal garbage truck. *"Bulaklak!"* the garbage man called back, standing on the running board above the truck's rear wheel and waving. He disappeared as the truck turned the corner, taking with it the clamor and stink of the city.

I was walking home along Joachim Friedrich Strasse, hurrying a little so I wouldn't be late for a date with my Indonesian girlfriend, Yayu. Life is too short. Life is too packed full of important duties: housework, the care and feeding of spouse and children, letters and thank you notes, and birthdays to remember, and on and on. When does a woman have time to care for her soul? I was looking forward to breakfast and an hour or two of heart-to-heart girl talk.

We had bonded, Yayu and I, amid the bustling life of this central European city of West Berlin. We'd found each other, down at the level of five foot nothing, down where all you see are backs and belts and bosoms. She had dark brown eyes and long straight black hair, as did I, and in the interminable, dreary Berlin winters, our faces became the lightest beige that we had ever known. We met at a party and gravitated toward each other. Her German was so much better than mine, speaking it everyday as she had to with her German physician-husband. My husband was an American singer. We lapsed into English whenever we could, whenever we could relax from the strain of speaking German. So English and German pushed further and further down into the depths of my soul the little Tagalog that I knew.

"You don't speak Tagalog? What about Ilocano? No? What kind of a Filipino are you?" Laughing, the other children in the embassy compound had run ran away from me. Those other Filipino children had slid easily from Tagalog to English and back, conversing in the fun-filled Taglish that I sometimes understood but couldn't speak.

English, English, English is most important preached my father. He was from Batangas, where Tagalog was spoken. Mom was from Pangasinan, where Ilocano was spoken. Growing up, I had no sense of where these places were. My parents had met at the University of the Philippines. My father spoke no Ilocano. His love letters to my mother were in English, the lingua franca on the campus of the University of the Philippines. As my brother and I were growing up, English was spoken at home unless my parents did not want my brother or me to know what they were talking about. Tagalog was their secret language. In our family, it separated the children from the parents. Raising my own children in West Berlin, I insisted that the children speak English, American English. I vowed that the two generations in our little family would not be separated by a secret language.

The city of Berlin today is united. The Wall is down. There is no East and West. The city's population is diverse. Shops and restaurants with goods and food from Asia, Southeast Asia, and the Middle East are now found everywhere. But in the 1970s, people from these parts of the world were viewed as exotic.

Where do you come from? Are you Chinese? Are you Japanese? When the war in Vietnam raged, the question was, Are you Vietnamese? I've been asked if I was Mexican and Mongolian. An acquaintance who had spent two years in Peru with Germany's equivalent of the Peace Corps swore that I looked like a Peruvian.

Finally, in the late 1970s, a woman asked me if I was from the Philippines. She could tell, she said, because her son had ordered a Filipino bride from a magazine ad.

Before hurrying to my breakfast date with Yayu that West Berlin summer morning, I had bought warm *Brötchen* (crispy-crusted breakfast rolls). Then I was in the flower shop, purchasing a small posy for the breakfast table when the florist presented me with a huge, fully open yellow rose. "For you, dear lady," he said with a bow. Oh my, how beautiful it was. As a regular customer, I enjoyed the special service and gladly accepted the gift.

A few moments later, I was overtaken by the clanking garbage truck. The garbage men had to jump off the running board, take their dollies to the central courtyards of the apartment buildings, affix the garbage cans to the dollies, and take them back to the noisy grinding truck on the street, where traffic was blocked by the gasping, odorous monster. With one swoop, the dolly was clamped on to a waiting arm, which opened the garbage can lid and emptied the contents into the truck's chugging belly.

On this day of the breakfast date with Yayu, the garbage man had called out to me, "*Guten Morgen!*" It was indeed a glorious summer morning. Sunshine speckled its way through the leafy trees. "*Guten Morgen!*" I called back, waving the bag of *Brötchen* and the yellow rose.

"Beautiful flower!" he called. I smiled. "*Sie sind die schöne Blume!* [You are the beautiful flower]," he shouted above the din. I, the thirty-something housewife, accepted the compliment with a nod and a tiny curtsy. Then the garbage man asked the question that sent me digging back through the years of memory.

"How do you say flower in your language?" He didn't want the English word *flower*. I knew that. He wanted me to say something different, something Asian, something exotic.

I thought of twelve-year-old me, reluctantly taking part in a Philippine pageant, when I didn't feel Filipino at all and the other kids laughed at me for not knowing Tagalog. I had to wear a *balintawak* (the informal country costume) when the older girls, the beautiful, *tall* girls, got to wear the sequined *ternos* (formal gowns). The pageant was staged by the Philippine Legation in Sydney where my father was consul general. The starched sleeves of the *balintawak* poked painfully into my armpits. The beautiful, tall girls were fair, and I was so dark. I couldn't help it—I loved to play in the sunny garden behind our house in Vaucluse. A double row of canine teeth poked out from my small face because the adult teeth were coming in on top of tenacious baby teeth. I felt so ugly, and I dared not smile.

We had to learn the words of the folk song. *Ikaw ay paro-paro.* (You are the butterfly)... *bulaklak*... something, something *ako.* I am the flower. *Bulaklak!* That's it! That's the word for flower. "*Bulaklak! Bulaklak!*" I called out in 35-year-old triumph to the gentleman from the Berlin Sanitation Department. "*Bulaklak!*" he echoed back as he and the truck disappeared around the corner.

Over breakfast Yayu and I chatted away happily as best friends do, then we turned our attention to an unhappy subject. "I'll pick you up for Dorothy's funeral tomorrow." Our mutual friend, Dorothy, the very same mezzo-soprano whose singing had turned a milling holiday crowd in a mall into a mesmerized, finger-snapping audience last Whitsuntide, had died suddenly the week before. Knowing how busy Yayu was, I offered to buy flowers for her when I bought mine the next day. "It doesn't matter what you get for me, but you must get seven different kinds of flowers," she said.

"Why seven?"

"In my country we have seven ceremonies after death. These help the soul pass through the seven stages before reincarnation," she explained.

Standing in the flower shop the next day, I decided that the different reds would clash with one another and purplish-blue flowers would not go well with some of delicate orange. Yellow was my favorite color, I reminded myself, so I told the florist to pick out seven different kinds of yellow flowers and make up two bouquets of seven flowers each.

"We should have talked about it more," said Yayu. "The colors are important . . ." I was driving down Spandauerdamm toward the Ruhleben crematorium, watching midmorning traffic and mentally screaming, "Ruth, how could you be such an ignoramus?"

". . . all written out in detail in the Tibetan Book of the Dead," Yayu was saying. I groaned. Me dabbling in things Asian. Me, cut off from my roots and slathering my path with cultural faux pas.

"It doesn't really matter," said Yayu, seeing my distress. "Dorothy won't mind."

The Ruhleben crematorium was in the British Sector, next to the British war cemetery and the British Army firing range. At the funeral, the minister's words were measured and passionless. In contrast, Dorothy's jazz trio, dedicating a short concert to her memory, played with the conviction, passion, and vitality of their departed friend. They played all of Dorothy's old favorites: *Georgia, Precious Lord, When the Saints Go Marching In*. There wasn't a dry eye in the chapel.

Nobody had ever known how old Dorothy was. From her long history in Berlin we knew that she must have been older than she looked. Now her birth date was printed on the funeral bulletin and quick mental arithmetic told us that she had been 30 when she had come to Germany to start a singing career; 43 when her first son had been born, and 58 when she had died.

Target practice could be heard behind the minister's words. But when jazz music filled the crematorium, heads started swaying, feet started tapping, until finally melodies from the New World, throbbing still with the heartbeat of ancient Africa, drowned out the stuttering artillery fire of British occupation forces nearby.

Eyes streaming, Yayu said, "That's Dotty's music, all right. She would not want us to cry though; she would want us to swing!"

Dorothy was the first of our American friends to die in Berlin. A friend's death makes people think about their own. For all those who live in a place that is not home, there comes a point when they must ask themselves a hard question: Where do I want to die? The fates may decide a place that is not your choice, but you have a right to state your preference. Berlin had been my home for a long time, but I was not at peace with the notion of dying there.

The city of Berlin itself, despite its separation from the rest of the West Germany, was refusing to die. Despite the migration of Berliners to West Germany, something new was opening. Right on schedule, Berlin's new International Congress Center opened in April 1979, although the letters of its name were still being secured in place minutes before the opening ceremony. A gargantuan project, costing DM 900 million, the ICC could simultaneously accommodate 20,000 people in 80 auditoriums and meeting halls. Would the ICC reawaken interest in Berlin as a conference center?

Charles and John were engaged to sing at 11:00 P.M. as part of the opening festivities. I went along to see the performance and the inside of Berlin's new silver giant. The performance took place in the middle foyer. While Charles and John sang and danced through a medley of old German songs, the rear projection screen above their heads showed Humphrey Bogart moving silently, earnestly, suavely, then passionately about Ingrid Bergman. On another screen to the right of *Casablanca*, Felix the Cat skidded in and out of quick adventures.

I had to keep reminding myself that I was in Berlin. This was an important opening that could help the city reach boldly into the future, despite its isolation. Bogart, Bergman, Felix, and those German songs belonged to another time, and yet they provided the setting for this new opening.

To my left stood an attractive young woman wearing a dress straight out of the early 1940s. She wore a white pillbox hat with a veil, which extended down to her upper lip. It was something my mother might have worn forty years before. I shook my head, but the vision remained. It seemed as though time was looping back upon itself.

From April to early June, the ICC was the site for *Der Deutsche Betontag* (Congress on Concrete Construction), *der Europaeische Brauerbund* (European Farmers Association), and the *Aerztekongress* (Physicians Congress). So many meetings and international congresses were being held all over West Berlin in the week of the ICC opening that every single hotel bed on the western side of the city was occupied. Springing at the chance to make money, East Berlin came to the rescue, offering hotel accommodations at top prices, to be paid, of course in Valuta, the name for one of the world's strongest currencies, the deutsche mark. East Berlin was not above harnessing the profit-making power of the decadent West.

In the years that followed, I would see the ICC twice a week as I drove over the Paulsborner Bridge, taking Scott to soccer practice in Zehlendorf. From the middle of the bridge, I could look across the freight railroad yards to the Funkturm (West Berlin's radio-tower landmark) and the New International Congress Center.

On weekends we'd drive to soccer fields and gym halls all over town for games and tournaments. With other parents, Charles and I would cheer along the Hertha 03 team, and often we'd hear the shouts of the opposing team's coach, "Someone cover the curly head! Cover the curly head!!" And I'd see Scott's thick curls bobbing among the straight fine flaxen of his fellow players.

At times, the soccer fields occupied the green edges of West Berlin. What to us were our city's outer edges were sometimes the innermost heart of Berlin as it once had been before it was divided.

One Sunday, I arrived at a playing field a whole hour too early. Scott was happy to watch the game scheduled before his, and I decided to take a walk. A group of six Turkish children were heading toward a park a block away. I headed that way, too. In the park, a huge sign told me in German, English, Russian, and French that I was leaving the American Sector.

My mouth went up into a crooked smile. The French verb *Vous sortez* should have been written in the subjunctive—that ghastly piece of French grammar that made us weep in high school. Not *vous sortez* you are leaving, but *vous sortiez*, you would be leaving—if there were no Wall. But here, hitting you in the face, here, unarguably, there was a wall, sheer, smooth, unscalable.

I had not seen the Wall in months. One did not go to see the Wall daily when one lived in West Berlin. When one had visitors, one took them to the showplace Wall, behind the Reichstag, which was in the West (our side), standing adjacent to the Brandenburg Gate, which was in the East (their side). The nonshowplace Wall of that Sunday cut through the inner city and went down a street of apartment houses.

A wooden staircase and platform had been built so that we could mount it and look over the Wall. Two men were already on the platform when I joined them. We exchanged Sunday morning pleasantries. They spoke with heavy Berlin accents, and they told me that they lived a few blocks away. They were out for a Sunday morning bike ride.

"Look at this Wall. It's twenty years old. It has walled them in over there. They can't travel abroad or anything," said the younger man. He was between 18 and 23. His rough hands told me that he was a laborer. His face was scarred, and his nose had been broken.

The older man, in his mid-forties, was thin and stooped a little with resignation. Both were friendly and polite towards me.

"I wasn't here in '61 when the Wall was built. I was in Africa," said the older one.

"Africa?" I was astounded. My prejudiced, stereotyped thinking would never have placed him in Africa.

"Yes, and in France."

"What were you doing in Africa?"

"I was in the French Foreign Legion. *Parlez-vous Français?*"

"*Oui, un petit peu.*"

In French, he explained that he had been in the legion for five years and returned to Berlin in 1962. No, he did not work; he had been invalided. He whipped out a battered identity card allowing him free rides on all public transportation.

"Actually, the Wall shouldn't be there at all. It is nonsense what they've done here," said the younger one in German.

We could see the guards in the watchtower peering at us through binoculars. Some one in an upper-story apartment poked his head out of the window. We wondered what he thought of us. The fifty-yard space between us we knew to be laden with mines and trip wires.

To our right in the park, we could hear the Turkish children squealing and laughing on the swings. Two children ran out into the open from the trees. They were playing tag right along the Wall. Then one chased the other back into the park.

We had nothing more to say to one another so, after several minutes of silence, we parted. The two men wanted to continue their Sunday bike ride, and I wanted to watch 22 little boys chase a soccer ball.

"*Tschüß!* [Berliner slang for 'bye]" called the young laborer, who, I suspected, was fond of fisticuffs.

"*Au revoir!*" called the erstwhile legionnaire.

"*Auf Wiedersehen,*" I said.

Later that month, I went for a midweek drive to the Teltow Canal, where the canal itself became the southernmost edge of West Berlin. The children were in school—Lynne now in ninth grade, Scott in fifth. This morning I was a liberated housewife and mother. I had space for thinking. And I reveled in the solitude, for at 3:00 P.M., I would put on my homemaker hat once more and become cook, nutritionist, maitre d', chauffeur, banker, plumber, and counselor. But for now—ah, for now I had a few moments for myself.

I left the car to walk along the canal. I looked across the placid water at the Wall of masonry along the opposite bank. I had not meant to come to the Wall; I only sought a peaceful place of beauty. I had seen the Wall many, many times before. This was one of the more beautiful stretches of Wall. Maybe I should say that this was one of the less ugly stretches. Its blank face seemed to observe me in silence. Sounds carried across water. I could hear the voices of the guards in the watchtowers in the East.

I strolled along the canal's edge and felt not confined but sheltered (sheltered from the oppression across the Wall). You could not get lost in this city, for its limits were well built. You could never take a wrong turn and end up in another place. No, you would eventually bump into the Wall. This Wall stood there straight and tall. It was honest.

Over there on the other side, people were oppressed and unhappy. Over here, we had freedom. How nice, how simple, when lines are clearly drawn, and you knew where you stood. There was a kind of safety in all that.

I wondered why they said that West Berlin was walled in, when we knew that the western side was free. They, over there, were the ones confined. How incongruous to be free in a place surrounded by a wall that did not wall you in, but walled out those who would come in. I thought about Robert Frost's words.

> Before I built a wall I'd ask to know
> What I was walling in or walling out,
> And to whom I was like to give offense.
> —Frost

I decided to sit on a grassy embankment beside an old bridge. Once, cars and trucks, bicycles and pedestrians had traversed this bridge, but now it was dotted with bright dandelions, growing happily in the concrete's cracks and crevices. In the not-too-long ago, people had crossed this bridge to go to work, to school, to meet friends. Now the bridge was closed, one end of it becoming part of the Wall.

The border guards could not see me now. I was far from traffic noises. In the distance a frog was croaking, a cricket was singing, flies were buzzing in the sunshine. It was warm and pleasant.

And suddenly, I was appalled at myself! I was appalled because . . . because I was not appalled. This was a border, an artificial border. It was an insult to human freedom! People had lost their lives trying to cross this border. There was even a memorial plaque to some poor soul who died trying to reach freedom right at this very spot. How did I dare to find this place pleasant?

Shouldn't I add activist to my list of occupations? Shouldn't I be marching in indignant protest? Shouldn't I be joining the crowd and raising my fist, especially when the international news cameras were nearby? Protesting crowds were less frequent in Berlin, but there was a constant sense of disquiet in the city. After all, the Wall was always there.

What had happened to that blithe young woman who once had seen all barriers, all differences, all limitations as challenges to be leapt over, defeated, overcome? Where was my winsome vitality, my winning youthfulness?

Was it possible that I was beginning to accept this terrible thing? Was the once youthful idealist admitting fatigue? Yes. You cannot be at war forever. How long can outrage last, when all you want is peace? Please, just let me sit for a moment—quiet and unappalled. Let me silently enjoy the sunshine and listen to the cricket's song.

"I think I'm going bananas. I need to get away from this city," I told Charles later.

Charles was all calmness, and I was agitation. "I'll talk to my travel agent in the morning," he said.

They chose a quiet spot for me, a castle, Schloss Gattendorf, that had been converted into a hotel. It was situated outside of Hof, just across the East German border in West Germany.

In all my seventeen years in West Berlin, I had never before taken a German train alone out of the city. With Charles and the children, I had flown in and out countless times, driven in and out several times since 1972 when my Philippine passport finally permitted travel through and to East Germany. But I had never traveled by train, alone, out of the city.

A throng of people in blue jeans on the platform at Bahnhof Zoo, West Berlin's main train station, crowded around one person. Charles recognized Bob Dylan who had performed in Berlin's Deutschlandhalle two nights before.

I shared a train compartment of six seats with an elderly German couple. They were Berliners. Now and then, the woman smiled at me. The train carried us swiftly from downtown West Berlin, past the Grunewald and Nikolassee, and into East Germany. We passed a playground full of waving children. Much later, near the West German border, we passed a field of female workers, all dressed in billowing skirts and wearing bandanas. They, too, had stopped their toil and were waving. I wondered who was waving out of our train.

Most of the journey was spent in silence and then at Hermsdorf, where the train stopped for inspection by the East German border guards, my fellow travelers started speaking.

This was where the two Germanys stared at each other in guarded silence. On the platform, the Vopos (*Volkspolizei*) patrolled the length of the train. They guided the long-leashed German shepherd dogs that had been trained to sniff out the undersides of the train. I could not imagine anyone daring to cling so dangerously to the bottom of a train just for a free ride into West Germany and freedom. But people must have tried it, or the Vopos wouldn't have been so diligently leading their dogs along the train's length. And their comrades wouldn't have been following along behind with low-slung mirrors held beneath the train in search of frightened, desperate people.

"*Tja,* terrible atmosphere every time we have to cross the border," said the woman.

"But what can we do?" said her husband.

Silence.

At the border just before reaching Hof, that familiar icy atmosphere again. We, in the train, had our border officials in gray and green, armed with walkie-talkies and revolvers. Outside the East German *Volkspolizei* in blue uniforms, automatic rifles slung over a shoulder, patrolled the platform. Germans staring stupidly across barbed wire at Germans. Brother against brother.

It was raining when I reached my castle and continued to rain solidly for the next two days. On Sunday it cleared up. On Monday it rained again. The view from my window of cropland and meadow, woods and copses, was pristine, so perfect and green that my urbanite brain had trouble accepting the reality of it.

For four days, I was the only guest at the castle. On Tuesday, a couple introduced themselves at breakfast. They had come to clear a piece of land they had just purchased. There were so many trees to be cut down. They had so much wood, they didn't know what to do with it all. It was even all chopped in lengths, ready for the furnace.

"What a pity," I said. "I know a lot of elderly people in Berlin who would love to have that wood. I see them all the time, picking up broken old fruit crates from the grocery stores and hauling them home for firewood."

"Oh, you are from Berlin! We are, too. But you know, there's nothing much happening in that city any more. We're Berliners, but we will move away eventually. In the autumn, we'll start to build our house on our property here. When the house is finished, we'll spend our vacations here. Eventually, we'll move over entirely," she said.

He said, "Not far from our property in the Fichtelgebirge there is a block of twenty-four flats under construction. Every single one of those flats has been bought by a West Berliner. Some West Berliners may tell you they will never leave Berlin, but many already have one foot in West Germany.

"All the major industries have pulled away from Berlin. Siemens used to be a big industry there and AEG [General Electric]. But no new investments are being made any more in the city."

The next day another couple checked into the hotel. They were Berliners, too. "Would you ever move away from Berlin, as that other couple are planning to do?" I asked.

"No, never. But that border running through the middle of the city is just terrible."

"Do you ever go across to East Berlin?" I asked.

He answered. "I have an eighty-five-year-old mother who lives in Weissensee [an East Berlin district]. If I could drive straight through, it would take me thirty minutes from my house to hers. But as it is, I have to process through the controls. I have to get a visa in my passport to cross over to the other side of my own city. It's crazy. It's like a foreigner going to another country. If my mother wants to visit me, her only son, she has to make an application four weeks in advance and fill out all sorts of papers.

"She's over sixty. She could come over altogether if she wanted to," I reminded him.

"She's says she's too old to move," he explained. "She's a stubborn old gal."

"What can one do?" asked the man, as I had so often heard Berliners ask before. "We'll just have to stay where we are and see what happens. Those big companies can move to West Germany, but you can't relocate a whole city. Can you?"

I spent the next days walking and swimming in the indoor pool, and pondering. If only they hadn't built a Wall. There was something so awfully insulting about a Wall.

On my return journey, I had trouble locating my seat on the train. A passenger, a Berliner by accent, was helpful. "Go ahead and sit anywhere. The train isn't full anyway," he said.

I had boarded at Hof. We were about to travel through the German Democratic Republic. I was returning to my home in West Berlin.

"Anyway," I said, as I chose a seat, "no one will be getting on between here and Berlin." He half-smirked, half-guffawed, then broke into a smoker's hack. He was an old man, going back to his home in West Berlin.

"You're right," he said, after he had recovered. "No one will be getting on anyway before Berlin."

I thought about his home. It had become my home, too. Our neighbors down the street were not free. They had to watch their words and their movements. Our job was to stay right there, like an irritation deep inside the Communist world.

Slogans on signs were flashing by my train window, all of them praising the value of Socialism. *Für das Wohl des Volkes. Mit der*

Kraft des Volkes. (For the good of the people. With the strength of the people.) *Technik und Produktion für das Glück des Volkes.* (Technology and production for the happiness of the people.) *Nur der Sozialismus garantiert wahre Menschlichkeit.* (Only socialism guarantees true humanity.)

Even though some people were deserting West Berlin, I had my doubts about whether Socialism was really succeeding. I knew that the Communist emperor had no clothes. Well, all right, maybe he had two coats. But both of them were beige.

I also knew that I was becoming a Berliner. The guest at Schloss Gattendorf had said, "Oh, you are from Berlin." He didn't take a second look and ask where I was *really* from. I didn't have to brace myself for the inevitable questions about my birthplace that I could not answer. He accepted me as a Berliner and wanted to talk about things he knew a Berliner would understand.

Back in Berlin, I picked up the threads of my life in the divided city once more.

"I really don't understand what all the fuss is, about the Wall I mean. If people want to come over, they could go to where the Wall ends and walk around it." The speaker was an American whom Charles had met on a visit to the States two years before. Now he was visiting us in our Berlin home, and we were having lunch.

Our mouths gaped. My staring eyes filled with tears.

"No, no, no," said Charles gently. "The Wall is not only through the heart of the city, it is completely *around* this half of it. There is no edge to walk around. We are encircled."

"So, can't they climb over it?"

"Not exactly. Besides border guards are under orders to shoot people trying to escape." Had the horror stories of foiled escapes slipped so soon from headlines and memories? "We'll take you to a museum, friend, then maybe you'll understand," we said. We wanted to take him to the House at Checkpoint Charlie, a museum of Wall escapes that described the many ingenious ways people had devised in coming over, under, and through the Wall. It documented how people had folded themselves into trunks of cars or worked for months to dig a tunnel. It was impossible to explain to him in twenty-five words or less the "modern border," which was three feet higher and stronger and smoother than the original Wall, with a pipe fastened along the top, measuring fifteen inches in diameter, that had been tested by East German athletes and proven insurmountable. These facts did not make for light and easy chatter over lunch. Unfortunately, our visitor never made it to the museum at Checkpoint Charlie. There were too many other important things to see and do during his short visit.

On the evening before the man's return to the United States, we invited him over for supper. He arrived half an hour late. "I got off the bus two stops earlier and walked. I was afraid I'd end up in East Berlin," he explained.

"It's quite impossible to blunder into the eastern section of town. There is this Wall, you see; and border guards and control points and . . . and . . ." Our words of explanation faded in our throats.

It dawned on us that this man might be one of millions who had no understanding of the Berlin situation, no idea that there was a whole city of two million people cut off from one and a half million people on the other side of the same city, and isolated from the rest of the free world. Our visitor was of middle age and college educated, yet uninformed of the geographical, historical, and political meaning of Berlin.

A week later, a letter arrived from Ohio. A neighbor of Charles's grandmother said her nephew, who was a private in the U.S. Army, was being sent to Germany. The neighbor did not know yet whether it would be East Germany or West Germany, but she would let us know soon.

" . . . let us know whether it is East Germany or West Germany? Oh, Charles," I said, waving the letter over my head. "She obviously doesn't have the faintest concept of how Germany and Berlin are divided."

Very carefully I wrote to her: "Your nephew will be sent to West Germany or West Berlin." I told her we would be glad to invite her nephew to our home if he ever visited Berlin. We would accompany him to Checkpoint Charlie and make sure he had a chance to understand what the city was all about. But grandmother's neighbor never wrote back, and we never knew whether the nephew ever came to the Divided City.

Not long after we had received that letter, people outside of Berlin were once again reminded of the city and its wall. On August 13, 1981, Berliners commemorated the twentieth anniversary of the building of the Berlin Wall. Newspaper and magazine articles, radio and TV programs, all presented fact-filled histories. Journalists and visitors from many countries moved about Berlin to see for themselves the Wall that divided a city and its people, their minds and their hearts. Wreaths were laid along the Wall where would-be escapees from the East had been shot dead. A demonstration demanding the fall of the Wall was held in front of the Kaiser Wilhelm Memorial Church, the solar plexus of West Berlin. On the eastern side of the Wall, meetings and demonstrations commemorated the rightness of the Wall, which had to be erected, they said, to stop the flood of people "so influenced by Western propaganda" that they left their homes.

And while newspaper stories about the Wall and its injustice were being written, ordinary people were doing ordinary things, living ordinary lives—going to work or to school, eating dinner. Somewhere at the back of their minds this date, August 13, and its importance were filed away.

On this day, 10-year-old Scott and I were visiting a friend who lived near Nikolassee, a crystal lake set in the Grünewald, one of the city's many forests. We decided to take a walk along the lake. We were a slow moving little band of people: my son and I; my friend, her two small children, and their dog. I held the toddler's hand. She was pulling a toy duck. My girlfriend had her baby in a bike seat, and she was walking the bike slowly beside us. Scott on his bike and the dog were far ahead of us. They came back to us, one running and barking, and one pedaling fast. They passed us and sped off into the woods behind us.

The woods were close and stifling. The crackle of gunfire reminded us that the U.S. Army firing range was nearby. We reached the lake and its coolness and let the children splash at the water's edge.

Suddenly, three, four, then five American soldiers in full combat gear went jogging by. Nobody was surprised to see them. Nobody said a word. We all knew Berlin was an occupied city, so no one even bothered to comment.

It was August 13, 1981, the Berlin Wall was twenty years old. Who would have guessed that in less than one year, Berlin would no longer be our home?

Charles and Ruth in their Halensee apartment

CHAPTER 6

Auf Wiedersehen

Two months later, Charles telephoned from New York. "We're moving back to the States!"

"Pardon?"

"I said, we're moving back to the United States."

The transatlantic telephone connection was without static, but I was having trouble grasping his words.

"You'll have to keep saying it over and over. I can't believe it."

Charles was in New York, rehearsing for a show that would tour Europe. The show's star, Julia Migenes Johnson, was under contract at the Metropolitan Opera and could not leave the city. Charles, therefore, had to travel to the Big Apple to rehearse. After so many years in Europe, Charles was now working in his own country, and he loved it. He loved it enough to want to move back.

A thousand questions leapt to mind, but transatlantic calls were expensive, and conversations short. I hung up and sat quietly for a moment. Then the questions came in a flood. How could we afford to move? Where would we live? What work would Charles have in America? How would the move affect the children? After twenty years of being a housewife in a European city, could I adjust? My ruminations faded in light of the gigantic task before us. I felt numb.

I thought of the cupboards I had partially cleared out in 1978. No half-measures now. I began to have dreams of the entire apartment building on Seesener Strasse, rising a full centimeter from its foundation, alleviated at last of two decades of Williams family accumulation.

In the past two years, Charles's deutsche mark earnings had remained stable, but the value of the deutsche mark against the dollar had risen. For civilians earning deutsche marks and paying the tuition at the American schools in dollars, the cost almost doubled. Public schools in America, we reminded ourselves with inward glee, would be free.

At first, we told no one of our plans. Christmas celebrations were beautiful, and I was already feeling nostalgic about them. I promised myself that we would re-create in America the thoughtfulness of Christmases in Germany. I telephoned Tante Susi more frequently and scheduled visits with her. How I cherished them. I departed quickly from each visit, not wanting Tante Susi to see my mounting sadness. I planned coffees, breakfasts, and evening meals with friends. I made the rounds, silently bidding them all farewell.

Ten-nine-eight-seven—I was pouring champagne into glasses, spilling some in my haste. Six-five-four-three-two—at the stroke of midnight our neighbor fired off a rocket from the balcony above ours. It was the first report heard on our street. All around me glasses were clinking and friends hugging and kissing.

Then I was toasting and hugging, being kissed and being hugged. I was used to that little hiatus, while my guests paid attention to partners first, then turned to me. It had become tradition for me to invite friends over for New Year's Eve. For the sixth consecutive year, Charles could not be home to watch the fireworks. I knew that on a stage in West Germany Charles was celebrating. During a pause in the late night performance of *Kiss Me Kate* in Cologne that night, players toasted in the new year.

Midnight. In an explosion of complete abandon, the West joined the East in celebration. The East, which had been blazing and firing already for twenty minutes, knew no respite. Flares and banners, multicolored bouquets of lights and rockets were shot higher and ever higher into the night sky. The cracking and boom and the scream of rockets crowded into my head. All of Berlin, a total area of 883 square kilometers, was in furious competition with itself.

Meanwhile, I stood with our children and friends on the balcony of our Halensee apartment, watching the other apartments along Seesener Strasse and on the other side of the Avus, the city freeway, go insane with fireworks. Every year, Berlin blew up thousands of marks worth of firecrackers and rockets in an annual new year half hour of midnight madness. And in the flashing and booming, that most well known of all lines, the border, the Wall, for this moment at least, was obliterated. Finally, at 12:30 A.M. on January 1, 1982, the insanity subsided.

As the smoke cleared along our street, the pungent smell of sulfur still hung in the air, evoking memories of hard fought street battles to retain control of an important freight train terminal nearby. More than three decades before, the shooting war had ceased, yet Berlin still held the dubious distinction of being divided like war booty by victorious forces.

Charles was on a five-week tour of West Germany. He would not be home for Easter. But Mama and Papa from Augsburg were visiting Tante Susi and Onkel Werner, so I invited Mama and Papa to spend the day after Easter with me.

Mama wanted to take a walk after lunch because she and Susi and their whole family used to live not far away and she wanted to have a look at the old neighborhood. Papa didn't feel like taking a walk, so we left him reading a magazine in an easy chair. The children had gone off with friends.

Mama and I walked to the end of Seesener Strasse, where it fed into Westfälische Strasse and the Kurfürstendamm. "This all used to be a large nursery for trees and shrubs, " said Mama. "They sold flowers here, too."

We crossed the Kurfürstendamm and headed toward the footbridge that took us across the Avus. Mama became a tour guide, pointing at this building and that one, speaking always of what used to be. We stood before the apartment building that had once been her home. "How run-down it looks. This was a beautiful street once, full of well-kept buildings," she said.

Was this the building where they had gathered in the cellar in a vain attempt to escape the marauding Russians? Was this where all that unspeakable cruelty had taken place? I didn't have the heart to ask the question. Mama wasn't recalling that chapter of her life.

In the building two doors away from Mama's home, a confectioner had lived. His shop had been on the ground floor, but his apartment had been on the third floor. His little daughter used to toss the small cakes and petits fours that were not perfect enough to sell off the balcony to children below. "There was always a crowd of dancing, laughing children in front of the house," Mama recalled.

We were about to cross back over the footbridge when Mama pointed at the freeway and the park on the other side. "This is where Luna Park, the big amusement park, used to be. Way back in the 1930s, we had a swimming pool there with a mechanically produced wave." A *Wellenbad* she called it.

So *that's* where Luna Park once was. I had heard Berliners refer to it often, but since I could not locate it on a map of West Berlin, I had always wrongly assumed it was on the other side of the Wall.

We were returning to our apartment when Mama said, "There is a cemetery around here." Her steps and her memory led the way. Sure enough, adjacent to the S-Bahn tracks there was a cemetery. I never knew it was there. Mama walked slowly up and down the rows of grave markers, recognizing some names.

I could not bring myself to tell her of our plans to leave Germany. She would find out from Tante Susi, and I would *have* to tell Susi soon. Mama was happily lost in recollections, and I just listened.

When we returned to the apartment, Papa was stretched out on the couch, fast asleep. How happy I was that he felt so at home. Had not Charles, when he was a young soldier, napped often on the couch of Mama and Papa in Augsburg?

I had baked a cake that morning for the afternoon coffee time. Quickly we prepared the table, then awakened Papa. I knew this would be the last time that I would have afternoon coffee and cake with Mama and Papa from Augsburg, and my heart was heavy.

A few weeks later, on May 2, 1982, I drove to Tegel Airport to pick up Charles. He was coming home from his last performance in West Germany before our departure from Berlin. How often had I driven this stretch of city freeway from our apartment in Halensee to Tegel Airport? Surely, by now, the car would almost be able to drive there all by itself? The spring sky was ever changing: rain cloud then sunshine; sunshine then rain. A flock of gulls wheeled darkly on my left, then arched to the right, the sun glancing off their white backs. My thoughts returned to that June day in 1963 when I had driven with a young U.S. Army captain to meet a planeload of journalists covering President Kennedy's visit to Berlin. This city freeway had not yet been constructed. We had driven along Teglerweg and on to Kurt Schumacherdamm, lined on that morning with barricades that would hold back the screaming crowds.

The freeway on which I was now driving led me away from the flock of gulls. Their squealing calls were being drowned out by the rat-tat-tat of an army helicopter slicing eastward across the sky.

I was driving through an underpass, the traffic all around me keeping pace. In front of me was a French military car with tricolor and army license plate. For a moment, I overtook it and saw a French officer in formal uniform staring stiffly ahead. Then the French car veered off to Napoleon Barracks.

The freeway rose, and now before me was the airport watchtower. Below and to the right I passed narrow gardens. Urban agriculture in peacetime; emergency food sources for the vanquished in the aftermath of war. I could see flowers and trees and running men in battle fatigues. Running men? Yes, running men, practicing the art of war in little urban gardens in case the city ever needed defending. There were no outskirts to this enclosed city. The big war exercises and maneuvers of the French occupation forces took place in West Germany and required the movement of large convoys across the autobahns. Here, within the city's Wall, French soldiers were being trained to advance by the meter.

As part of the maneuvers, a smoke bomb had been released. Bright pink smoke drifted ahead to the huge electronic board listing plane arrivals and departures. And at a crosswalk I saw a school teacher shepherding a class of youngsters across the busy thoroughfare. One of the children was pointing at the red smoke. How would the teacher explain it?

I was upstairs in our neighbor Sigrid's living room. The burden of decisions pressed heavily on my shoulders. We were trying to find a date for the Sommerfest. I realized I probably wouldn't be doing this with Sigrid again. We'd watched our children grow up together. Charles had brought our sound asleep four-year-old daughter up to Sigrid at 3:00 A.M. on the morning when my contractions were suddenly three minutes apart. And Sigrid had put Lynne in bed with her sound asleep five-year-old son.

Over the years, we'd struggled with coal buckets and ashes together. We'd told each other of specials at the supermarket. And now she wanted to know our summer plans.

"I don't know when we will be in Berlin. I don't know if we will even be in Germany . . ." Suddenly, I was sobbing.

Sigrid and our other Berlin friends were sadden by the news of our departure. Why were we moving? We were leaving for the sake of the children, we answered. We were leaving because it felt right. Blank stares. Heads shaking. No understanding. Were we sure we should do this? Why were we turning our backs on them? That question hurt.

Our American friends were excited for us and organized farewell parties. For our neighbors in Halensee, we planned our own party to say good-bye. Friends in the U.S. Mission asked us to invite some of our closest Berlin friends to a farewell dinner in their home in Dahlem. We finally told Tante Susi and Onkel Werner, and they were among the guests of honor at this final dinner in West Berlin. They could not believe that we were actually leaving. "I am shattered," said Onkel. "I'm sure you've thought this through," said Tante. I just wanted to hug them and hug them. We'd be back, we promised; now our West Berlin friends would have an excuse to visit us in the States.

We were invited to a party in East Berlin with several friends from the West. Detlev and Ursula would be coming, too. We knew that this would be the last time we would make the crossing over to the eastern half of the city before our move. As usual we telephoned Detlev and Ursula to let them know that we were on our way.

"We're leaving now. We'll start crossing the checkpoint in twenty minutes." How carefully routine our wary little game had become, how devoid of detail. Never forget that someone could be listening.

The day was cold and drizzly, as we, West Berliners, used the various crossover points into East Berlin. As usual, Charles and I crossed at Checkpoint Charlie. It had become our checkpoint, a kind of namesake. A Yugoslavian couple also drove over at Checkpoint Charlie. Two West Berlin couples took the city train. Their crossing was delayed because one woman had forgotten her passport, and she was required to buy a temporary passport, complete with photo, which was taken on the spot. Another friend was fined 300 deutsche marks for attempting to carry over several cassettes of recorded music. The cassettes were confiscated. A West German woman and her Lebanese husband drove over at Heinrich Heine Strasse, the auto crossing point for West Germans and West Berliners. The border guards searched their car thoroughly, making them remove the backseat so that they could inspect the space behind it. Nothing subversive was found.

When we gathered, we were sharing stories of our short journeys from the western side of the city. *Ja-ja,* the usual hassle. How familiar. So annoying. You'd think we'd get used to all this by now. Laugh—what else could we do? We felt constrained and a little hysterical. We were going to make the best of it. We were going to enjoy ourselves because no one, no system of politics—no WALL—could stop us.

Mingled with unuttered angry thoughts was simple pleasure. How good it was to see one another. Sixteen of us crowded into the living room. Many in the group were singers. One belonged to the Don Kossaken Choir, known for programs of Russian folk songs. He needed no prodding to perform. The man from Yugoslavia had brought his guitar. Tonight's abundant live music would dispel our anger over the confiscated cassettes.

The buffet was spread carefully on the bed and desk of the room adjoining the living room. We sang and laughed and told jokes and enjoyed good food. Charles sang in Hebrew an Israeli folk song, *Hine Matov*, based on Psalm 133, "Behold how good and pleasant it is when brothers dwell in unity." And the hours tiptoed by.

Political jokes flew thick and fast. "Did you hear about the time when Erich Honnecker [leader of East Germany] awoke one morning to find himself all alone in East Berlin? Everyone had escaped to the West. He wandered about the city until he came to the Wall. And there he found a note that said, "Erich, don't forget to turn out the light."

We laughed and hooted. Vodka was poured into tall tumblers. And we toasted again and again. Life was sweet and bitter, joyous and terrible. We all joined in singing passionate love songs, while the host and hostess continued to replenish empty glasses. Suddenly, the music's tempo changed, and we seemed to be charging across the endless Russian steppes at a desperate gallop.

A young woman of German-Russian parentage had brought her accordion. She had spent several of her childhood years in Scotland, spoke English with a Scottish burr, and loved singing folk songs from her former home. She was leading us all through a rollicking chorus of " . . . the bonny, bonny banks of Loch Lomond," when someone pulled back a cuff to check the time.

Ursula inspected the pendant watch hanging from her neck: 11:30 P.M.

Soon we would have to leave. We would have to get back across our various checkpoints before midnight. Our visas were only valid until then. We had to prepare ourselves to cross that border once more.

We became serious—and tender—and, at the same time, angry again. The gall, rising within, began to choke us. This was ridiculous. But the unarguable facts remained. Someday, someday, perhaps we'd be able to visit one another without getting visas, without border controls, without the barbed wire and concrete—and maybe even stay as long as we liked, as long as we chose. Tears glistened. How many more years would we have to live with the anger that engulfed us all? When would Detlev and Ursula ever be able to visit us in the United States?

But now—there really was no time to think about all this. We had to hurry. We had to leave. Handshakes and hugs were warm and long. We had to say good-bye. Just one more hug. One last *Auf Wiedersehen.*

Auf Wiedersehen. Das Wiedersehen means the seeing of something or someone again. With our eyes set toward the States, with our lives consisting of boxes and cartons, I was unexpectedly called to the Philippines.

The invitation from the Philippines that arrived in late spring of 1982 was more of a summons. My mother and father were celebrating their fiftieth wedding anniversary. The letter, written in my mother's own hand, stated clearly that I, I *alone,* was invited to come and join the festivities.

"She *still* doesn't include you and the kids in the family," I said. Despite the passage of time, my mother retained a cold politeness toward Charles and the children. But Charles's heart is wider than the world's. He held me at arm's length and looked into my eyes. "Your mother and father are active and still healthy, but they are old. You should go." Well, if Charles could forgive them for not accepting our marriage, so could I.

In Manila, our visits to some of the city's fine eateries was fun. I was chauffeured around, shown off by my proud parents, pampered by maids. The manicurist clucked at my neglected nails. The astonished cook rolled her eyes when I requested dried fish and rice—a typical Philippine breakfast—and refused toasted white bread and eggs. I preferred the breakfast of the maids.

Anniversary celebrations were held in Mahabang Dahilig, the little barrio in Batangas in central Luzon, where my father was born. We drove along the new superhighway that connected Manila with Batangas City, then followed a potholed, bumpy road for a torturous hour until we reached Mahabang Dahilig. The village people were gathered in the road to greet us. My uncle Djoni kissed me, presented me with some baby pictures of me and my brother, then burst into tears.

Here I was with a whole village of people who looked like me. My height. My hair. My skin. I wasn't different. I wasn't exotic. But I was still a stranger. They would be watching my every move.

My second cousin Rufina invited me to her house. It was just down the road a bit. Rufina was exactly my age. Rufina's father had never left the barrio, nor had she. My grandfather had sent my father to school in another town, and that was the start of my father's remarkable life's journey. I looked at Rufina and thought about our fathers and the different decisions they had made in their lives. Rufina had never left this little barrio, her home. I had never before been to this barrio, and I had no home.

When I told my mother that Rufina and I were going to Rufina's house, my uncle started shouting adamantly, "*Maputik! Maputik!* You cannot go. It is far too muddy!" I was learning the Tagalog word for muddy.

Never in my life had I ever let a little bit of mud deter me. In fact, the thought of a muddy challenge tantalized me. I insisted on going despite the mud. Uncle dispatched a contingent of three cousins to ensure my safe passage through the mud to Rufina's house. I was, by now, more curious about the mud and the house than ever.

The end of June in the Philippines is well into the rainy season. Steady rains and an occasional monsoon cloud burst had been drenching central Luzon since the week before. Indeed, just prior to inviting me to her house, Rufina had taken refuge from the rain under the eaves of my uncle's house.

Rufina and I and the three other cousins started down the narrow barrio road, whose potholes were all filled to the brims with fresh rainwater. Soon the going became treacherous for much of the gravel on the road had been washed away and the potholes were mud puddles. Finding a firm footing became a chore. A shower gave cooling relief to our physical efforts of fording and leaping and dodging. No matter how I zigged or zagged, strong arms supported me and an umbrella was held so that not one hair of my head would get wet.

We left the road and started up a muddy hill. "*Maputik! Maputik!*" I called out, exhilarated at learning a new Tagalog word. "*Maputik!*" cried a chorus of cousins, all hovering close and somewhat fearful. I knew why they were so concerned for my safety, for if indeed I had stumbled or soiled my skirt they all would have been held responsible.

One third of the way to Rufina's house, my shoes were so caked with mud that I could hardly take another step. I looked at this soil—Philippine soil, rich pitch black, and sticky. Its origins were volcanic. I wanted to bend over and let it ooze through my closing fists. I wanted to taste it and rub it all over my face. I wanted to make mud pies and fling it about me like a wild thing. But looking at all those relatives, supporting my hands and arms, I saw concern in their eyes.

So I feigned a slight stumble and left both shoes stuck fast in the mud, and continued barefoot up the hill. Gasps and laughter all around me. Gasps and laughter. And then just laughter.

"Well, I can't put those on anymore," I announced. More laughter.

Someone pulled the shoes from their muddy grave. Now my feet were in the mud. It was smooth and soft and warm. It was sticky and slowly slippery and black, black, shiny black. I was fascinated. I pretended at every fourth step to falter, but I was feeling, feeling, feeling through the soles of my feet—my land, my country—for the very first time, the land of my birth.

"Oh, Ate Ruthie," said a young cousin.(*Ate* is the term of respect for an older sister), "you will get mud under your toenails. Then Auntie [my mother] will know that you have been barefoot."

"I don't mind," I said freely. Their looks of utter consternation, however, told me that they minded, they minded a great deal. In the days to follow, I was to learn how feared my mother was by the family.

At last we reached Rufina's house, and an order was barked to fetch the boots. I was led to the water tank. I was supported while someone washed one foot and then the other; while the mud was scraped from under each toenail, while one foot was dried then directed into a blue rubber boot, then the other foot.

I clomped about the muddy hill outside Rufina's house, snapping pictures. This was a really real nipa house—a bamboo house, up off the ground, just like in the postcards. We went inside, where I was allowed to shed the boots.

Inside it was cool and wonderfully airy. A tiny, ancient, feeble woman was making her way down the four steps that led from the raised sleeping space.

"My mother," said Rufina. I held the back of her mother's hand to my forehead, a sign of respect toward elders. Rufina told her who I was, but she did not see or hear well. On a little platform beside the stairs was a man dressed in shorts and T-shirt. He was playing solitaire with an extremely worn-out pack of cards.

We went to the kitchen and dining area and then to the outside porch, where the dishes were washed and set on the bamboo wall to dry.

"My mother is very old. My brother is retarded. Those are my responsibilities. I am not married," said Rufina. She stated all this with acceptance, satisfaction, and simple contentment.

One cousin announced sadly that we had better start back, Auntie might get worried. I wanted to kick off those awful boots now heavy again with clinging mud. But I had already caused a lot of work to get me into them in a clean condition. So those boots and I struggled back down the hill, and I wondered when I would ever again touch, feel, or even see the Philippines.

My brief excursion to the tropical world of flashing smiles and laughter, mangoes, papayas, and roast pig was manna for my rootless soul. And it was the last time I would see both my parents alive and healthy, for my mother would die seventeen months after my visit and my father's funeral would follow a year later.

One week after my return to Berlin, we said farewell to the city.

On the morning of departure day, the buyer of our baby grand piano came to pick it up. It was our prize, our baby. But its sale paid for the plane tickets that would take us across the Atlantic. I watched from the balcony as Charles and its new owner supervised its loading onto the truck. Charles shook the new owner's hand and hurried back upstairs. There were still a million things to do.

The next day, after one last trip upstairs and a final look around at the apartment already filling fast with the new tenant's furniture, we climbed into a rented VW Sirocco and headed for the checkpoint that led out of the city.

This was the last time we'd be going through checkpoints. We all knew it and were silent.

"Visa, please," said the boarder guard.

"We are registered residents of West Berlin. We need no transit visas."

"She does!" He pointed at Lynne. He waved Lynne's passport at us. Then, miraculously, he relented. "She's over 16, make sure she gets a transit visa or has registration next time you travel through the German Democratic Republic!" He gave us back our passports and waved us through. We rode on in silence, grateful that the guard had chosen not to insist on regulations.

Ahead of us lay our last European summer: six weeks in Salzburg, where Charles would teach and direct at the Susi Nicoletti Workshop on the American Musical. It proved to be just the right psychological hiatus we needed. With the wrench from Berlin behind us, we enjoyed summertime in Salzburg, where the greatest musicians from all over the world converged. We were gypsies, living out of suitcases in two rooms of an Austrian pension at the foot of the Unterberg.

On August 25, 1982, we drove to Frankfurt, turned in the rental car, then boarded a plane for the United States of America.

We chose to move to the Washington, D.C., area because so many Berlin friends, both German and American, had settled there. They would be our support system during our years of adjustment to life in America. We would all be working away at carving out an American space into which we could fit. Three of us had been born outside of the United States. Only Charles was a born-in-America native. Three in the family carried blue American passports. The children were American because of Charles's citizenship. I was an alien; a fact that made our twelve-year-old son double over with mirth. All of us spoke English not quite with an accent, but in a way that made people look at us thoughtfully and then ask where we were from.

We found that people in and around Washington, D.C., had important lives and hurried about accomplishing important tasks. Friends lived so far away from one another that impromptu parties were out of the question. And few had time to enjoy Sunday afternoon coffee and cake. Sunday afternoons were devoted instead to watching football on television and mowing lawns. But the greatest shock to our viscera and wallets was the discovery that freelance performers could earn only one-tenth to one-third as much as their German counterparts. At the toughened age of 43, I would have to find employment.

At one job interview, the prospective employer said, "So you lived in Berlin before coming to the Washington Area. East Berlin or West Berlin?"

"West Berlin."

"Er, is that *our* side?"

When our first Christmas in the United States was at hand, I was in a post office buying stamps for Christmas letters to friends in Berlin.

"East Germany or West Germany?" asked the postal clerk.

"It's West *Berlin*," I said.

"It has to be East Germany or West Germany," she said. I didn't think the postal clerk wanted to hear about the technicalities of how World War II had not quite come to closure in Berlin.

"Well, all right then," I said, "West Germany." I silently asked my Berlin friends to forgive my blasphemy.

In 1986, I became a U.S. citizen, at last. I was a copy reader at Time-Life Books in Alexandria, Virginia, and was at my desk on the day after taking my oath of citizenship. At 2:00 P.M., Marfé Ferguson, one of the other copy readers, announced that all should put down their pencils and celebrate the new American. I was surprised and delighted. Someone made popcorn. Someone else gave me an American flag, and a third presented me with coupons for two free McDonald's hamburgers. I was in!

Time flits by swiftly when you are learning so many new things at once. By 1988, six years after our arrival in the United States, Scott had graduated from high school; Lynne had graduated from the American Musical and Dramatic Academy in New York City; Charles had made his Metropolitan Opera debut as Sportin' Life in *Porgy and Bess;* and I had bounced around through five jobs— clerk, secretary, administrative assistant, copy reader, marketing director, and secretary again.

We had arrived in America with a bundle of cash and owed nothing. Now we were heavily in debt, making payments on a house and two cars. But it was, we were assured, the American way.

To celebrate Scott's high-school graduation, we had promised him a trip back to the city of his birth. Charles was performing in

Berlin, and that summer Scott and I joined him. Although Charles had crossed the Atlantic several times since 1982, it would be the first time back to the Divided City for Scott and me.

Berlin was the same old city I had known so well. The Wall running around it seemed as solid as ever, its eastward-facing side thickened still by mined death strips, barricades, and watchtowers, and patrolled by guards and German shepherd dogs.

On closer inspection, West Berlin had changed in some important ways. In 1982, little children had just discovered what an inviting surface the Wall was and had written love letters on its blank face. A valentine, pierced by an arrow, was drawn above the words *Lieber Peter* (dear Peter), written in childish script.

In the intervening six years, the Wall had evolved into a graffiti gallery and a space for colorful Western political expression. The icy atmosphere near the Wall had changed to something like a carnival. Souvenir stands, flags fluttering, were selling film, postcards, T-shirts, and little replicas of the Wall. And the empty lots near the Wall where war ruins had been cleared, but nothing built, were now parking spaces for buses, disgorging tourists who later stood before the Wall having their pictures taken and not knowing whether to smile or scowl. Good old Berlin—why not transform a dreadful thing into a tourist attraction?

Berlin's yellow double-decker buses were often covered with advertising now and not so clearly identifiable, especially to the city's aging population. "Buses have a duty to be yellow," one elderly Berliner complained to me. Who would have imagined that Berlin's dependable yellow buses would one day become mobile billboards?

So many friends now drove and were eager to show me their new cars that I hardly had to use the public transportation system.

My former English pupils had grown up. Some were married and had children of their own. I had become a great-auntie many times over. How proud I was.

And in Tante Susi's apartment, the coal ovens had been replaced by central heating

Traffic was heavy, especially on the city freeways. The Ku-damm Karree, the one-time flea market, was now a beautiful shopping mall where business was brisk. But faintly, ever so faintly, above the bustle, I imagined I could still hear echoes of a jazz beat and the lilting mezzo-soprano voice of my friend Dorothy.

A neighbor took me to see Steinstuecken. The Wall on either side of the road leading to the enclave was overgrown now by vines and shrubs. Only the upper third of the Wall, with its 15-inch pipe fastened on top, stood bare. Nature was overtaking the barrier and clothing it in green.

Friends invited us to spend one afternoon on their small yacht. We drove to their mooring in Heiligensee, then boarded the craft for an excursion down the Havel. With East Berlin on our starboard side, we looked over the water to the buoys that marked the border of the two halves of the city. In drenching rain, we sailed past the large cruise ship *The Moby Dick*. We looked to the East where the shore was marked by the Wall, not so easy to see now beneath the vines and creepers. Here and there I could see places where the Wall had crumbled.

Later in the afternoon the curtain of rain lifted, and the sun dared a peek under the lid of clouds. On reaching the Greenwich Promenade, we turned around and headed north, the eastern border now to our port side. At the wharf once more, our hostess performed magic, pulling out plates of food and goodies and all sorts of drinks. The sun hung low over the trees, over the watchtowers. The evening sky turned gold and pink. The rain clouds of the morning were only shy shadow players now in the panorama of the sunset. Trees and watchtowers stood in stark silhouette. Watchtowers?

Sonnenuntergang ist im Westen, nicht wahr? (The sun sets in the west, doesn't it?)

"Ha-ha! That is the East over there. We are watching the sun set in the East," said our host. And we all smiled that special smile of West Berliners. We were enjoying once more the ironies of the Divided City.

Had the Berliners become gentler? Or was I tougher? I'd been in Berlin for two weeks when I realized that I had not yet been scolded by anyone. Scott had bought a pair of trousers that he took back to the shop the next day because they were too tight. The salesperson waved lazily in the direction of the clothes rack, and without a word or the slightest hint of fuss, the trousers were exchanged for the next larger size.

One Saturday afternoon, I went for a walk all by myself along the Kurfürstendamm from Adenauer Platz to the Kaiser Wilhelm Memorial Church. Beside the little kiosk on George-Grosz Platz, I noticed new benches for sitting and several new telephone booths. At the kiosk, I picked out five postcards and was steeling myself for the bark of the salesperson inside the kiosk when a small voice said, "Three marks fifty." The voice of the man inside the kiosk was so soft I had to read his lips. I left him in a kind of daze and continued my walk.

Suddenly, I was in the middle of a jostling crowd. Music from a Dixieland band filled the air. Ah, of course, it was the first Saturday of the month; the shops would be open until 4:00 P.M. Shoppers were milling around clothes racks set out on the wide sidewalks, crammed full of merchandise at bargain prices. These shoppers seemed to be dancing to the music. Aware of the music on some half-listening level, melting to the rhythm of the beat in the very air they were breathing, the shoppers, the walkers, the crowd all seemed to be dancing. Dixieland on the corner of Joachimsthaler Strasse and the Kurfürstendamm and the whole world was dancing, even the people sitting at little tables and drinking coffee or Berliner Weisse (beer) with green Waldmeister syrup. And the music was Dixieland.

A black mechanized gorilla held reign on this corner, moving like clockwork and intriguing the children who came to stare up at him, but I was remembering a man in a gorilla costume that used to work this corner. Little children were often afraid of him, but tourists had their photos taken with him.

I went into one shop after another, full of clothing, jewelry, accessories, porcelain. So much choice, so much merchandise, and found myself suddenly at Breitscheid Platz, at the Kaiser-Wilhelm Memorial Church. It was crowded with people, especially young people—blue jeans, blue jeans, everywhere blue jeans. It was a carnival ground of people who loved to look at other people. A man with a rubber face put on a pair of oversize spectacles and pulled faces.

I thought back to the days when the 10A bus made its tortuous slalom way past this place, when it was still a deep excavation and the Europa Center was still blue lines on paper. Every day on my way to work at the Press Center, we passengers on the bus would watch the progress of the excavation and the construction. And then I remembered even further back, before there was a Europa Center, when a Ferris wheel spun above the earth that was yet to be paved.

"Aren't you Mrs. Williams?" a voice called out to me in one shop. "Yes," I said hesitantly. The saleswoman's face was familiar, but I couldn't put her in context. It was especially embarrassing since she seemed to know almost everything about me. How were the children, she wanted to know. She knew Lynne and Scott by name and only after my careful questioning did I learn—or remind myself—of the names of her children. Our children had played together, at our house or theirs. They were grown up now and scattered, and she was divorced from her African-American husband. Her boys had gone to live with his relatives, but they felt unwelcome in the States and returned quickly to Germany, where they were more at home.

Something else was new. The people were not staring at me. I, the Asian woman, was no longer exotic. I looked around and saw many faces that were not German: Asian, Turkish, black Americans, Africans. People from all over the world now lived in West Berlin, many of them owning businesses and restaurants. Berlin had become an international metropolis. How wonderful it was no longer to stand out as a foreigner. I thought of signs I had read in the subway, signs on the platform and in the train carriages, signs showing faces of all colors and hairstyles, that called for all Berliners to be kind to one another.

At a flower shop, I stopped to admire the bright blooms set out in buckets on the sidewalk. The little lady florist came out, deep in discussion with a young man who followed behind. She was short (my height), fiftyish, and round, with a white apron that hung below the hemline of her dress. She was very serious about her task.

The young man wore a gold earring. His hair was purple and yellow and stood in stiff peaks. His arms jangled with many bracelets, and his greasy jeans seemed to have been painted on his body.

Ah, I thought, she's going to scold him and send him packing. But they were utterly focused on their mission. Together, they considered this red rose and then another. Together they carefully picked out five red roses. (Flowers are given in odd numbers in Germany; even numbers are considered bad luck.) The little round lady and Mr. Punk then chose the greenery to complement the bouquet. These two generations of Berliners were engrossed completely in choosing the right flowers. They didn't notice me or the world about them.

Yes, there was an ease about the West Berliners that pleased me, and the gentle fragrance of affluence filled the air. West Berliners, the most widely traveled of all Germans, had used their good earnings to escape the bonds of concrete and journeyed abroad. In their minds, experiences, and cameras, they had brought back impressions from the far-flung reaches of our globe. And their city reflected their newfound tastes. My island had become cozy. The Wall of Shame had become—dared I admit it?—a Wall of Protection, protection from all those people on the other side who wanted to come over. What might they do when they got here? We did not know that the cocoon would soon burst. An invasion was about to take place, not by the Russian tanks that for so long had lurked close by, but by people on the other side of the Wall, hungry for the affluence and wealth they had seen in pictures. They called it freedom. They had yet to learn how freedom was not without a price.

A year after Scott's and my visit to West Berlin, in the summer of 1989, the rolls of barbed wire that marked the barrier between Hungary and Austria were gathered up and hauled away. East Germans began crossing the border into Austria and from there into West Germany. By the end of October, East Germans were entering West Germany at the rate of 1,000 per hour. People were crossing a once-restricting border because it no longer held them in and they were curious about life on the other side. As in the summer of 1961 just before the Wall went up, people were on the move again.

Lynne had found work performing at the Kammerspiele Theater in her old hometown, and in October, I planned to visit her. Little did we know that the dates for my trip would mark the end of an era.

Was this young woman performing on stage the little child who had once delighted us with her antics? "Save it for the stage!" Charles had said, when later the teenage Lynne became dramatic.

She had listened well to her father's words and had become a performer like him.

What fun I was having visiting old friends again, but how different the atmosphere in the city was from what it had been just 14 months before. There was a hard to define feeling of great changes about to take place. I asked whomever I visited the same question: What did they think about the thousands of East Germans coming over to the West every day? Without exception, the answers were the same. Well, in principle, of course, yes, they should come over. But, but we already have a critical shortage of apartments. Where will we put them all? That question remained unanswered, and other questions percolated upward from the depths of the country's soul.

Over dinner one evening, Sepl and Inge and Petra remembered how in the 1970s, Charles and I had taught them "facies," jokes involving the face. In answer to my question about the East Germans, Petra pressed her nose with her open palm and said, "Don't you think we'll all have to stand a little too close?" Howls of laughter.

Two days later, I thumbed through my old address book, found the number in East Berlin, and dialed. Would they be home? It was hard to believe that seven years had passed since those long, warm hugs of farewell in 1982.

A young man's voice answered the phone. He remembered me and gave me his mother's phone number at work.

"Ruth!" screamed Ursula. "It's a good thing I'm sitting down, or I'd probably fall over."

"How is everyone?" I asked. Something kept reminding me to watch my words. I was talking to someone in the *East*. Her phone might be tapped. I wanted to ask why they hadn't joined the westward stream of humans coming over, but I knew the question could wait until we were together. Ursula invited me for afternoon coffee on the following Sunday.

"I'll come over Checkpoint Charlie at 2:00 P.M. Will you meet me?"

"Of course."

I telephoned Tante Susi. What gifts should I take over to the East? "Take coffee, chocolate, soap, and chewing gum," she said.

"Wait a minute," I said. "That's what I used to take way back in 1974."

"That's the point. Things haven't improved."

"No wonder they're coming over," I said. But I wanted to take my friends more than just coffee, chocolate, soap, and chewing gum. There had to be something more special than that. I would bring the world to them, symbolically at least.

On the first Saturday of November 1989, Karstadt, a department store in the Wilmersdorf District of West Berlin, was offering special bargain sales in its newly renovated food department. The crowds were bustling but not shoving. If they couldn't find what they were looking for in this store, it would be found in the next store—if not today, then tomorrow. Prosperity had softened West Berliners' manners, and there was an ease about them that pleased me. How different from the days when memories of wartime scarcities gave shoving power to their shoulders and elbows.

I joined the crowds in Karstadt's food department on Saturday, November 4, and bought kiwis from New Zealand, mangoes from Puerto Rico, wine from Spain, dates from Iraq, avocados from Israel. That evening I watched news reports of peaceful demonstrations in East Berlin's Alexander Square.

The next day, I went over to the East. Ah, yes, Checkpoint Charlie. How familiar. Hi, CC, remember me?

As in years past, I had to exchange twenty-five deutsche marks—at the rate of one to one—into East marks. My bags were inspected, but I didn't have to declare the money I carried.

"Oh, so *that* is a kiwi and *that* is a mango," said the border guard. She was actually polite.

Detlev was waiting for me on the other side with a small bouquet of flowers. I was eager to see Ursula, but Detlev was obviously in no hurry to get home. With my arm around his waist and his around mine, I found myself locked into his brisk short-striding gait, watching the pavement slide by as he insisted on pouring out information. He started telling me his whole life's story.

"This revolution is a revolution of our youth," he said. And he would repeat this statement many times during the afternoon.

"I've resigned from the Party because of the beatings and bloodshed during the antigovernment demonstrations last month. I'll let you read my letter of resignation when we get to the apartment. I had joined the Party so I would know the enemy better, but last month's atrocities were too much for me. [Some weeks before, antigovernment rallies, begun in churches, had been brutally crushed by riot police.]

"I've been engaged in this revolution for fifteen years. We all have code names and we only know one other person in the underground network, so we have little to reveal in case any one of us gets arrested."

Detlev went on and on, urgently telling me as much as he could before we reached the apartment. My goodness, I thought, all this intrigue and subterfuge going on while I was watching our sons play tag around the monoliths of the Pergamon Museum? Code names and clandestine activities while I was forced into buying ten erasers and ten bottles of glue?

"I've always admired Angela Davis," said Detlev.

Huh? Angela Davis?

"What I admired about her so much was her courage, her courage to speak out against things in her society that she found wrong. We had no woman in our country back in 1970 who had courage like that. She was a victim of the Cuckoo Clan," he said.

"That's Ku Klux," I corrected him.

"No, cuckoo is better," he said. I felt like smiling, but I heard weariness in his voice.

I remembered how he and Charles used to have animated discussions about the difficulties of being an artist in the East and about how he longed to express new ideas.

"I can't tell Ursula what I do. Whenever I attend meetings or work with the network to produce our literature, she thinks I am at my studio. I don't tell her anything. In case I get arrested, she can honestly say she knows nothing."

As on visits to the East in the past, there were pauses in our conversation: silence until approaching pedestrians passed by; silence in the elevator when we were not alone.

Finally, we reached their apartment. Ursula looked much the same as she had seven years before. How old were our children now? Their two sons were twenty-five and eighteen. My children were twenty-three and eighteen. We remembered how our young sons had played soccer together; how our husbands had discussed politics, how we women had talked about houseplants and soap.

We recalled how I had brought them drip-grind coffee, only to learn that they couldn't get a filter holder anywhere in East Berlin. They remembered how on my next visit, I came with a porcelain one. And they pulled it out of the kitchen cupboard to prove that they still had it.

Their younger son, Peter, arrived with his girlfriend. He wanted her to meet me. We chatted briefly, and then they left.

"What do you say to all the people from the East going over to the West?" I asked.

"I don't blame them, especially the young people. Actually, I worried a little that our older son might be among them," said Ursula.

Their older son, Jens, was seated to my left. "Would you go to the West?"

"If I could go just for a visit. Just to satisfy my curiosity, I'd go," he said.

"Of course," said Ursula, resurrecting an old saw, "we can always wait until we are sixty." We laughed, but the laughter this time was brittle with smoldering impatience. Little did any of us know on that Sunday afternoon, November 5, 1989, that just four days later they all would have a chance to satisfy their curiosity about life in the West.

Jens said he had a job and his own apartment. He also had a girlfriend, and she had her own apartment. As they were not sure

how their relationship might develop, they wanted to keep sepa-
rate apartments for a while.

I thought of Lynne, now sharing a one-bedroom apartment
with four other young artists on the western side of the city.

"Remember," I said, "how our four children sat on this very
living-room carpet and watched television together? Is it still true
that teachers question their pupils about what they watched over
the weekend, and if they watched Western television, the family
gets reported to the State Security Ministry?" I asked.

Ursula answered, "They used to do that, yes. But not any
more. What I find most exciting is that we can watch our own East
Berlin news programs now."

I didn't understand, and my face must have shown it.

"They never reported any news before," said Detlev. "They
used to talk about the coffee cups on the table and the hats the
women wore, but they never reported the real issues or what actually happened. And the programs were so dull. No wonder everyone here watched the television from the West. We always explained
things to our sons but warned them not to talk to anyone about
what we discussed."

Ursula added, "Our TV programs are now reporting what's
happening. Watching our own East programs is a whole new experience. All we want is freedom to speak our opinions even if they
are different from the official line. And I want more than one party
and a chance to choose and vote."

"Democracy is sometimes a lot of work," I said." The people
must be responsible for deciding many things. I just mailed off
my absentee ballot because I won't be home for the elections
on November 7. I had to mark my choice not only for state
governor but also for three other officials. And I had to vote yes
or no for the use of public money for such things as a library
and a prison."

They just looked at me wordlessly, clearly unable to comprehend. Their faces reminded me of the gray surface of the Wall
surrounding our city, the surface that had stared blankly toward

the West for years, the surface before it had evolved into a bright, brash mural.

"The most ardent wish of the youth in the G.D.R. is to be able to speak openly and honestly," said Detlev. I couldn't argue with that. "What we want is the freedom to have a different opinion," repeated Detlev.

"Then what would you say if a group like the cuckoo clan , as you call them, decided to express its ideas in your country. That's a different opinion, too," I said.

"Oh, no, that would be wrong," said Detlev.

I explained to them that there were lawyers in the United States who would work to defend the right of the cuckoo clan to express their opinions, even though the lawyers themselves did not agree at all with them.

Again, blank stares. The Wall had done its work well. I felt a widening gap between us and a growing sense of panic for there was so much more to discuss. I wanted to tell them that freedom meant freedom for everybody and because of that things can become chaotic. I worried for them and their sacred Germanic sense of order.

For a brief moment, I yearned for the simple, safe, warm hugs that meant we would stay friends and survive separation despite outside political ideas.

But the afternoon was slipping by. It was time to present the gifts. From my shopping bags, I pulled out the fruit and explained where each kind had come from. They handled and smelled each one. But they didn't express that childlike joy that had given us so much pleasure when we brought gifts over in the past; they just kept repeating, "We don't have things like this over here." I had the sinking feeling that I had committed some mistake. Was I after all just reminding them of their deprivation? Was I rubbing their noses in the things they *still* could not obtain?

I had a ticket to see the new musical comedy at the Theater des Westens and curtain time was 8:00 P.M. If I could cross back at Friedrichstrasse instead of Checkpoint Charlie, I'd be so much closer to the theater, and thus able to visit a little longer.

"One used to have to return over the same checkpoint. But so many things have changed. Do I still have to do that?" I asked. My East Berlin family didn't know. Oh, how embarrassing. How could they know that?

As their Hungarian neighbor upstairs crossed back and fourth routinely, Ursula suggested giving him a call.

"No," said Detlev, "someone might be listening."

"Don't be silly," said Ursula. "They don't do that any more."

"You never know," said Detlev and went upstairs. He returned saying I had to go back over Checkpoint Charlie.

Before the last good-byes, Ursula said, "Tell them over there in the West that we just love Alf."

I blinked. "Alf?"

"Yes, we love his show. He is so cheeky. He speaks his mind. He has the guts to contradict everyone and everything. We really like him over here."

"Alf?"

I waved to them as I made my way through the slalom course of barricades and gates. And they stood, as always, on the other side, waving.

I thought of all those past visits. Of the television pictures from the West: Kermit, Miss Piggy, *Little House on the Prairie* and its little lessons of right and wrong. And now they liked Alf, the extraterrestrial of unabashed tongue.

On the following Wednesday, November 8, I was walking along the Kurfuerstendamm on my way to meet Lynne. I would be flying out of Berlin early the next morning, and we were to have our last meal together.

I was thinking again about the silences: those pauses in the conversations with friends in the West that signaled their uncertainty about the future, and the uncomprehending silences of my friends in the East.

A fine mistlike rain was falling, and the unusually mild autumn had suddenly turned cold. The lights along the Kurfürstendamm captured the veil of raindrops in haloes; and dark shadows played around street lamps and moving headlights. The first strings of Christmas lights were lit. I had a premonition that next weekend this place would be bustling with people. I was sure of it somehow. I saw the boulevard crowded and noisy. Then, I saw torchlight glancing off rows of dark helmets, and soldiers marching in two long columns of four.

"Please, Mom, stay just two more days. I want you to come with me to the party on Saturday night," pleaded my daughter.

"Sorry, honey, but I have one of those really discounted tickets. I just can't change my departure time." I couldn't explain it, but I had such a sense of urgency; something seemed to be driving me out of the city.

On November 7, the border guards' orders to shoot to kill anyone trying to cross from East to West had been canceled. I left my walled city on the morning of November 9, 1989. East German authorities could no longer contain the crowds of people converging at checkpoints around the city. Charles greeted me at National Airport in Washington, D.C., with the words, "The Wall has been opened, and people are coming over from the East." We embraced and looked into each other's eyes and, wordlessly, embraced again.

On November 10, Lynne telephoned from Berlin. "There's so much happening! Everyone is so happy the Wall is coming down. Before we started rehearsals today, they opened a bottle of champagne, and we toasted. Then after rehearsal, it took us two hours to get home. It usually takes fifteen minutes. What a jam! Oh, and Mom, all the buses are letting the East Berliners ride for free. And taxi drivers are offering free rides. And all the bars and cafés are serving free drinks to the visitors. McDonald's is giving away hamburgers. And on the radio, people are calling in and leaving their names and addresses saying, 'We're having a dinner party and we have room for thirty-five people and we'd like to invite any East Berliners who can come.' Isn't it great?"

"Sure is, honey," I said.

I thought of myself at twenty-three, arriving with Charles in West Berlin in 1962 and of how the city had captivated us. Now Lynne was calling from Berlin, her home, and talking excitedly about events in the city. How happy I was for her, for this was her home. Although we had chosen to leave, we were once again caught up in the vibrant energy of the city.

Over the weekend of November 11 and 12, 1989, the streams of East Germans crossing into the West turned into torrents, and stories of tearful humans filled front pages and television screens all over the world. Each major U.S. television network sent reporters to broadcast from the Wall, while champagne-drinking Berliners cavorted behind them, dancing on top of the Wall or sitting astride it.

Friends who had lived in Berlin for two or three years during our two decades in the city telephoned from all over the country to rejoice with us over the news from Berlin. One phone call even came from Japan. People whose friendships we had made since our move to the States called to somehow participate in the celebrations. Maryanne Stoessel, whose husband, Walter, had been U.S. Ambassador to the Federal Republic of Germany, called us, inviting us to a "Hooray there's a hole in the Wall party." At it, we met again so many people we had known in Berlin. We talked in incredulous fragmented sentences. Wasn't it great? The Wall is actually being torn down, as we speak. Who would have thought it would happen in our life time? We caught ourselves looking at each other in disbelief.

On Monday, I was back at work, and a coworker asked, "How was your vacation?"

"Great. I was in Berlin."

"Where's that?"

"In Germany."

"Oh, I see."

But it seemed to me she didn't see anything at all. "Berlin. You know, the city with the Wall," I prompted.

"Wall?"

"Yeah, you know. It's been in the news."

"Well, I haven't really been following that. A wall . . . hm . . . is it like the wall in Jerusalem? Does it have a religious significance?"

"Not really." I was beginning to hyperventilate. I had to leave the room. At lunchtime, I took a walk along the banks of the Potomac at the northern end of Old Town Alexandria. The Potomac River is wide, but you can see Maryland on the opposite banks. There never were buoys floating down the center of this river, buoys that marked a border between two countries. There never was a wall on the opposite bank that prevented us from seeing into Maryland.

The young woman who didn't know about Berlin reminded me of myself so many years before: a young person too busy with her own little life to pay attention to screaming headlines about a faraway city called Berlin. I lived in America now, I had to remind myself; in this country, one is free to ignore world events. But oh, how I ached to tell her some things she had not heard.

CHAPTER 7

Without the Wall

In May 1990, both Charles and Lynne had engagements in
Berlin. Charles was performing the role of Sportin' Life in the Theater des Westens production of *Porgy and Bess.* Lynne was still engaged at the Berliner Kammerspiele. So Scott and I flew from Dulles
Airport in Virginia to Tegel Airport in Berlin for a family reunion
in the newly transformed city of Berlin; Berlin, the city *without*
the Wall.

Now that the Wall had been breached, it seemed that all we
wanted to do was go to where it no longer was or where new crossover points had been set up. People were moving through these
crossovers in crowds of giggling young people, groups of laughing
elderly people, buses and cars full of people from Poland and Ro-
mania who were coming across to shop for goods they could never
before buy so easily.

Charles and I were like a young childless couple once more,
exploring our city. We walked hand in hand through the Tiergarten,
the city park that had once been a royal hunting ground. From
there, we walked across to the Brandenburg Gate, where just months
before television cameras had recorded a city in celebration.

But now, there was no Wall.

On either side of the Brandenburg Gate, the city's most famous landmark, the Wall had been dismantled and hauled away
like some unnecessary bulky trash. A bald swath of earth ran along
the ground, scattered about with litter from the two systems of
economy that once had held the Wall in place: crushed empty

packets of East Germany's Karo cigarettes, empty cans of Coca-Cola and Sprite. The swath was a pathway now, and we walked along it in silence.

The next day I called a friend who lived near the Tegler Forest at the northern end of West Berlin.

"Hey, Jennifer, do you have any Wall left?"

"Yes, there's quite a large bit just behind our house."

"May I come and try to chip some off? Do you have a hammer and chisel? I hear the city has run out of chisels."

"We have hammer and chisel and whatever else you might like. Let's make a day of it. We could go for a walk. We could walk across to the East. There's a new crossover point close by."

"How much for a visa?"

"I don't know. I haven't even been over yet."

We went to the Wall with chisel and hammer and chipped some pieces off and put them into a plastic bag. Then we went to the crossover point, and the border guards just waved us through. We paid no money for our stroll into the East. No money exchange. No passport control. No questions asked. It was effortless, and our pace slackened to match the ease of it all.

Ruth chips off some pieces of the Wall

Jennifer's home was in the French Sector, and just on the other side of the former border were barracks for Russian soldiers. We came upon a low stone wall enclosing a grave site where three Russian soldiers lay buried. Each headstone was clearly marked with a red star. We could not get close enough to read the names or dates, but we knew somewhere three mothers must have grieved for them.

A friend of Scott invited him to play soccer with a West Berlin team against a team in the East Berlin district of Koepenick. Scott traveled with the team across to the East. Charles and I caught the train to join him, crossing over at Friedrichstrasse. We paid five deutsche marks for the visa.

The S-Bahn platform was crowded with Romanian women dressed in colorful skirts, all talking excitedly, fanning themselves because the weather was so warm. They were carrying huge boxes of stereo radio-cassette players.

We asked the East Berlin platform official if we were on the correct platform for the train to Koepenick. He was friendly and assured us that our train would arrive in seven minutes. He was middle-aged, his uniform neat, the hammer-and-divider symbol of East Germany clean and clearly visible in the center of his hatband.

A Romanian man, burdened with packages and perspiring profusely, hurried toward us. "*Wo Friedrich Strasse?* [Where Friedrich Strasse?]"

"*Das ist Friedrich Strasse!* [This is Friedrich Strasse!]" Our official shouted at him as though he were deaf.

"*Wo Friedrich Strasse?*"

"*Wo wollen Sie hin?* [Where do you want to go?]"

Without answering, the man and his packages retreated.

"Oh, I don't know what the future will be," said the East German official. "So many foreigners. So many foreigners. You are all right. You speak very good German."

But I remembered how years ago, German officials had shouted their instructions at us when our foreignness and ignorance of the German language had offended them.

We were invited to a party, and guess who was there? Detlev, Ursula, Peter, and Jens. We hugged and laughed and toasted. And no, they had had no problems driving over into the West.

But amid the jokes and banter and good food, there were pauses in our merriment, moments of thoughtful silence. We were all remembering parties in the East. And here we were—together in the *West*. And we weren't sixty years old yet. Detlev and Ursula, and Peter and Jens and their girlfriends had simply driven over, no visas, no inspections, no paperwork. Often, we caught ourselves just looking at each other in disbelief.

The lure of Berlin was stronger than ever. The next spring I returned: 1991, thirty years since the Wall had been built, thirty years since my wedding day, thirty years since Charles in an open army jeep had been greeted with flowers and cheering Berliners as his army unit rolled into the city. This time, my traveling companion would be Margaret, a coworker in job number six in my restless, relentless search for enjoyable work in the United States.

Margaret was planning a trip to Poland via Berlin. She was going to visit her mother near Breslau and wanted to buy a color television for her on the way. It's not Breslau, it's Wroclaw, Margaret kept correcting me. Change, change, Europe is in a constant state of change, I mused. Wroclaw became Breslau became Wroclaw. But Berlin remained Berlin. Or so I thought.

During the previous twelve months, the two Germanys had become one, and the country was grappling with the problems of adjustment to its newly united self. We read stories of how unwelcome Poles and citizens of other former Eastern Bloc countries had become in Berlin, especially because they were crowding the stores, buying huge quantities of food as well as radios, televisions, and stereo equipment.

"How ironic," I told Margaret a day before our departure. "I am Asian, but I am perfectly at home in Berlin. It is the Poles who are being treated so badly in Berlin now. We will always speak English; maybe the Germans won't think you are Polish. Don't worry, I will make sure you get from the plane to the train safely, and I know where we can buy that color television for your mother. I know Berlin very well," I said. One should always be careful of boastfulness.

As soon as possible after landing in Berlin, we bought the television, then went to the main train station at Bahnhof Zoo to buy Margaret's ticket to Breslau. All trains out of Berlin left from the Bahnhof Zoo station; I had lived in the city long enough to know that fact well.

"The train for Poland leaves from Lichtenberg at 5:40 this evening," the ticket seller announced.

"Lichtenberg?" I had never heard of Lichtenberg. I hesitated. And into my uncertain silence, the ticket seller shouted, "You go in the direction of Strassberg and get off at Lichtenberg! Lichtenberg! Direction Strassberg!" They were all new place names to me. I understood every word he yelled, and his impatience and annoyance stabbed me. I had reverted to an ignorant foreigner again.

I studied the map. Oh, *East* Berlin. Well, the city was all one now, of course. Of course—one city, not two. No more Wall. Try to remember that, Ruth. Lichtenberg was in East Berlin, sixteen city train stops from where we had stashed our luggage. I hadn't learned yet to think so big. New Berlin, greater united Berlin, was twice as large as the city I had known. Remember, Ruth, that the dear old Berlin you once knew so well was only half a city. I allotted 90 minutes to reach Lichtenberg.

We made good time until we passed Friedrichstrasse. The moment the train crossed the border-that-is-no-more, we could have walked faster than the train was moving. When at last we reached Lichtenberg, the Breslau train was already waiting at the station. We ran down the stairs, across to the adjacent platform, and up the stairs in time to watch the train pull away. The next train to Breslau would be in 24 hours.

I had to keep calm, and I tried to be cheerful. First, I wanted to call Ursula, maybe we could put the TV and Margaret's suitcase in her apartment overnight and not have to haul them back and forth across this huge—my goodness it had become huge—town.

But the few phones we found had been vandalized or had long lines waiting to use them. We were in the main hall of the station, passing a café in which sat three young men. They stared at me coldly, then they gave me the finger. I answered their gesture by blowing them a kiss. It was a moment of recklessness, I admit, but hey, we had been traveling nonstop for 26 hours, our jet-lagged bodies were moaning with fatigue, and now we had missed the train.

The three got up from the table and approached me. "*Was heisst das?* [What is the meaning of that?]" They towered over me and hissed. I felt no fear for they looked just like my former English pupils. Had I not known so many like them? They were Berliners by accent, tall, ruddy, and strong. They would have been blond, had their heads not been shaven.

"*Was heisst das?*" They asked again.

"I blew you a kiss. A kiss is a sign of love." The teacher in me was articulate and sure, and my German was flawless. There was a small pause.

One of them had biceps bulging under his leather jacket. He planted his feet firmly apart, drew his hand across his scalp, and declared proudly, "I am a Skinhead." My calmness seemed to irritate them. "*Heil, Hitler!*" screamed the second one, raising one arm in stiff salute.

One in dirty jeans and leather boots said, "I have a wife who is far more beautiful than you." Get a grip, little boy, I'm old enough to be your mother. "I'm happy for you." I kept my reply soft, for I was slowly beginning to realize that we might be in danger. As though we had rehearsed it, Margaret remained silent.

"*Heil, Hitler!*" said the third one, saluting. And then, "You slanty-eyed foreigner, get out of Germany!"

Sorrow filled me: sorrow of a depth I had never known before, utter and complete: sorrow for the young people on the western side of the city who called me Tante; sorrow for the generations before them that had endured so much on both sides of a reinforced concrete Wall; sorrow for the country that once had been my home; and sorrow for these three benighted young men who were so wrongly and dangerously directed.

I saw the long arm of history reaching back and back. I wanted to say, "Please, please fellas, don't start with *that* all over again." But I was overtaken at last by prudence and remained silent. They would not understand my real intent.

One of them began to push and shove me. They ignored Margaret completely. The second young man followed me, kicking the suitcase I was pulling on a luggage cart. He kicked and kicked until the luggage cart broke. That seemed to satisfy him; he stopped, and we got away safely.

The next day, an American friend of many years brought Margaret and me by car back to the station in Lichtenberg. We gave ourselves two and a half hours to travel from the western side of town. We allowed plenty of time to get lost in the poorly signed streets of the eastern side of the city, whose traffic lights were still not timed to accommodate the quadrupling of traffic that had occurred since the Wall had come down. On our circuitous search for Lichtenberg station, we passed West Berlin taxis stopping and turning around, winding up and down the tiny streets that surrounded the station; other West Berliners were lost in this newly acquired part of their city.

"Why did the train go so slowly once we crossed the border?" I asked my friend.

"They have to. The tracks, the rails, even the sleepers are in such disrepair, they must travel very slowly to be safe," he explained.

After Margaret had boarded the train bound for Breslau, er, no Wroclaw, I could prepare for my visit with Lynne, who was performing in Luebeck.

How proud I was, when just 48 hours later, I was watching our daughter on stage in a production of *Nunsense*. It was in the very same theater where Charles had performed his first production of *Porgy and Bess* 17 years before. It was my first visit to that lovely seaport. Its charm and tidiness did not disappoint me, but my view of the city, now in light of my encounter with young Hitler-saluting neo-Nazis, was burdened by the role I knew the city had played in World War II, the war that had aimed so long ago to end National Socialism.

Luebeck was the first German city to go up in flames under the British bomber command in 1943. It had no armament factories or heavy industry. Luebeck's buildings, dating back to the Middle Ages, were made primarily of wood, and the sight of an entire city ablaze was intended to send a wave of dread across Germany. My three young bald "acquaintances" may never have heard of this. Would they be destined to learn the hard way that the world will retaliate against Nazism, as in the past?

I spent my last week in Germany back in the once-Divided City, visiting and telephoning friends. "What!" Ursula screamed over the phone. "You were in the S-Bahn . . . with a Pole . . . and a television . . . are you crazy? I don't even ride the S-Bahn anymore; it's too dangerous. People have been terrorized in the S-Bahn stations. One person was thrown out of a moving train." (A week after my incident, a Polish man was stabbed by Skinheads at Lichtenberg station.)

"Why didn't you tell me about these things?" I asked Yayu, who had welcomed me to her home.

"If I had told you all the changes in the city in the last six months, you would not have believed me," she said calmly. "I don't read the newspapers anymore. I don't like to watch the news on television. It's too depressing."

Most reactions from friends in West Berlin were by way of dry discourse. "Well, of course, you have to understand these Nazi sentiments were repressed under Communism. That was *one* good thing about the Communists. But now all these things are allowed to come out." I would hear half a dozen versions of that explanation. Yes, freedom, the freedom at last to express opinions formerly suppressed had been gained. But I don't think that is quite what Detlev had in mind when he yearned for freedom just five days before November 9, 1989.

Many guest workers in East Germany had come from Vietnam. They were like the Turkish guest workers in West Germany. My Skinheads probably thought I was Vietnamese. When the West German government took over, many East Germans lost their jobs, but some guest workers were allowed to keep theirs because their work contracts would soon run out, and they would be sent back to their own country. For now, at least, some of the guest workers were better off than many East Germans, and there was a lot of jealousy.

I did not know that Vietnamese people had come to live in East Berlin as guest workers. Could I expect those young hairless ones to know that I, someone who looked Vietnamese to them, had become part of the life of the western half of Germany's greatest metropolis? I think not. That concrete Wall had kept us apart and ignorant of each other.

On two successive evenings, I went to concerts. At the Chamber Music Hall of the Philharmonic, I enjoyed string quartets of Schumann and Brahms, performed by members of the Radio Symphony Orchestra. The next evening, I drove quite easily, barrier free, past the Philharmonic and across Potsdamer Platz to the Platz der Akademie, where the Berlin Sinfonietta was playing Bach and Mozart in the small concert hall of the Schauspielhaus.

I remembered Ursula's words of longing back in 1978. "Someday it will be the most beautiful of all centers of culture." Well, it was beautiful all right. Its interior pink walls and murals echoed another century; German culture at its worthiest. The Platz der Akademie lay like an island of light surrounded by the usual darkness of poorly lit East Berlin streets.

A few days after the concert, I joined a group of friends and acquaintances for a short trip on the cruise ship *Europa*. We cast off from the lake, Wannsee, in the southern part of the city and sailed south. Along the banks the Wall had been removed in several places. We peered into once-forbidden territory and saw front lawns and backyards, people sunning themselves or hanging out washing.

We sailed to the Glienicke Bridge, that notorious bridge of Cold War intrigue where spies were once swapped. Glienicke Bridge had once been the edge of our world. I remembered how my family had watched cruise ships on the western side of the border sail up to Glienicke Bridge, turn around, and go back. But now we sailed *under* it, hooting and hollering like children, for sounds echo with full resonance under bridges, and our spirits were bursting with joy. And then we were quiet, for before us stood Potsdam, the former royal residence of Frederick the Great. I remembered how our family had stood at the edge of our city where Glienicke Bridge connected to West Berlin, and from there we had gazed across the waters at Potsdam. But now *Europa* was sailing past Potsdam through Templiner Lake and on into Schwielow Lake. I was so excited. I called out to my fellow passengers, pointing at tall buildings and spires, "What is that? And what is that?" At first they could name some structures, but as we proceeded farther into the former East Germany, they shook their heads and grinned. "We're strangers here, too. We don't know what that is."

Someone pointed out to me a gentleman I guessed to be in his seventies. "That's Norbert Schultze. He wrote the song *Lili Marlene.* You've heard of it. It was a very famous song in World War II."

"Of course," I said. "The band is playing it now."

Later, as our ship was moving slowly down a narrow canal, I found myself seated next to the venerable Mr. Schultze. He looked at me thoughtfully for some minutes, and then he asked, "*Was verschlaegt Sie nach Berlin?*"

I could not answer him right away because that verb *verschlagen* carries with it all sorts of meaning. On the surface, Mr. Schultze's question was, "What brings you to Berlin?" More deeply, *verschlagen* connotes: What winds of fate have redirected your life's course and brought you to Berlin?

"Well . . . when the Wall was built, my husband's United States Army unit was sent to Berlin."

He said nothing at first, just continued to regard me without speaking. All of my years of learning about this fascinating city, this country, and the people who gave it breath and spirit seemed to crowd into that long moment of silence: the Polish doctor who wept on offering us bread and salt and water; Hans and his strange black glove; Mama and her wonderful plum cobbler; Papa and his quick laughter; Tante Susi and her unflagging optimism; Onkel Werner, his kind humor and twinkling eyes; Professor Garay and his guidance; Sepl, Inge and Petra; so many wonderful meals and warm welcoming homes; so many witty and generous friends in the West; Ursula and Detlev in the East, who persevered despite shortages.

On the cruise ship *Europa*, Mr. Schultze said finally, "Oh, that long ago, when the Wall was built."

"Yes," I said. "I was on my way to America. We planned to stay just one year."